Geography

& Maps Activities

INTERMEDIATE

Intermediate Geography and Maps Activities

Editorial Contributors: Laurie Borman, Carole Wicklander, MaryClare Goeller
Illustrator: Scott Burroughs
Maps: Rand McNally GIS department
Product Management Director: Jenny Thornton
Designer: Pam Krikorian
Design Production: Erika Nygaard
Production: Carey Seren
Artwork by Shutterstock Images

Printed in U.S.A.
April 2016
PO# 45850
ISBN 0-528-01544-3

If you have any questions, concerns or even a compliment, please visit us at randmcnally.com/contact or e-mail us at: consumeraffairs@randmcnally.com or write to:
Rand McNally
Consumer Affairs
P.O. Box 7600
Chicago, Illinois 60680-9915

randmcnally.com

Maps are flat drawings of different places on Earth, such as a country, a state, or even your neighborhood. Maps tell you where things are located, but you have to learn how to read them first.

The key to reading a map is the **legend**, which appears on most maps. It contains clues called symbols that help you find things. **Symbols** are little pictures that stand for something on a map, such as a road, lake, or town. Can you find the legend for the map of Glenwood Campground below?

GLENWOOD CAMPGROUND

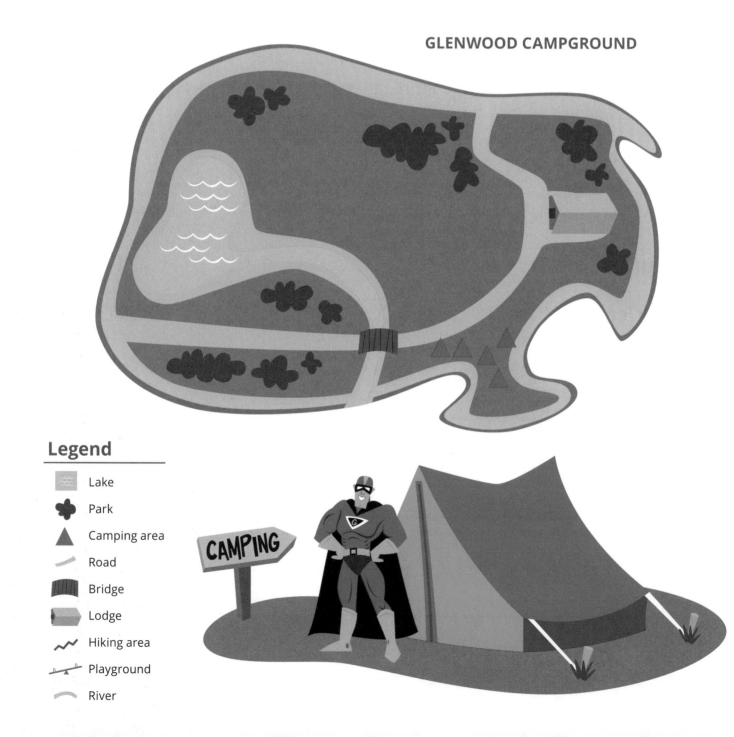

Legend

	Lake
	Park
	Camping area
	Road
	Bridge
	Lodge
	Hiking area
	Playground
	River

What's missing on the campground map? The mapmaker made a mistake and forgot to put all of the symbols from the legend on the map. Look at the legend and the map on the opposite page and spot what's missing. Then draw the missing symbols on the map.

You can figure out exactly where the missing symbols go by solving the riddles below. Write the names of the missing symbols on the lines.

1. Put on your boots and travel past the lake. These rocky trails will make you quake.

   _____

2. Between your tent and the lodge you don't need a guide; just look for the swing and jump on the slide.

   _____

3. Across this you must run, from your camper to the park, to have some fun.

   _____

Create a legend with symbols that might be included on a map of your city. Some things you might include are streets, schools, and parks.

Legend for a map of _____

A **compass rose** isn't a real flower, but it sort of looks like one. Its "petals" point to north, south, east, and west. These are called **cardinal directions**. Some compass roses also show the **intermediate directions**: northeast, southeast, northwest, and southwest. If a place on a map is both north and west, the direction is northwest. What direction is a place that is both south and east?

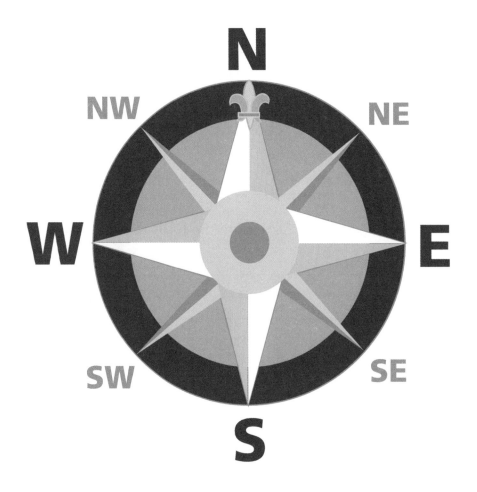

Who Knew?

Follow That Butterfly!
Monarch butterflies have their own built-in sense of direction that helps them get where they're going. Maybe one of the flowers those butterflies have been hanging around is the compass rose!

Use the map and compass rose to find your way around Arbor Heights Elementary School.

1. You enter the front door. Which direction do you go to get to the school office?

_____

2. Now you have to deliver a message to the librarian. Which direction do you go?

_____

3. You move on to the sixth-grade classroom. Do you go southeast or southwest?

_____

4. It's time for lunch. Which direction is the cafeteria from the sixth-grade classroom?

_____

ARBOR HEIGHTS ELEMENTARY SCHOOL

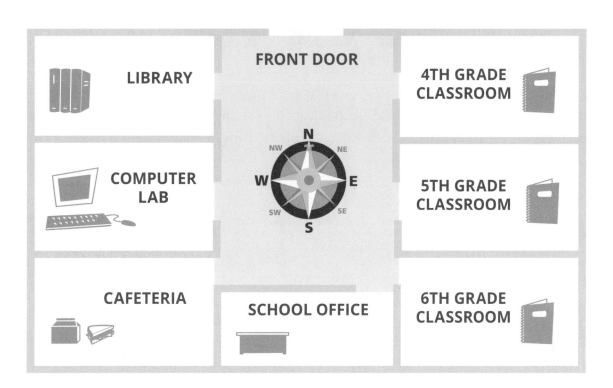

Map grids help you find things on a map. Grids usually have a row of letters or numbers going across and a column of letters or numbers going down the side.

Using these letters and numbers to locate things on a map is a little bit like playing bingo. In fact, the grid locations are called **bingo keys**. Each letter and number on the grid creates a square, such as A1, E3, F2, and so on. Look at the grid below. What shape is in square B3?

Imagine a grid on a map. Instead of looking for a shape, as you did in the grid above, you can look for cities, roads, airports, and other things.

 **Who Knew?**

Lost and Found
The first world map to have "America" labeled on it was created in 1507. The map was lost for more than two centuries! It was discovered in a German castle in 1901.

Road trip! Test-drive your knowledge of the map grid and use the bingo keys to make your way around the state of Colorado.

COLORADO

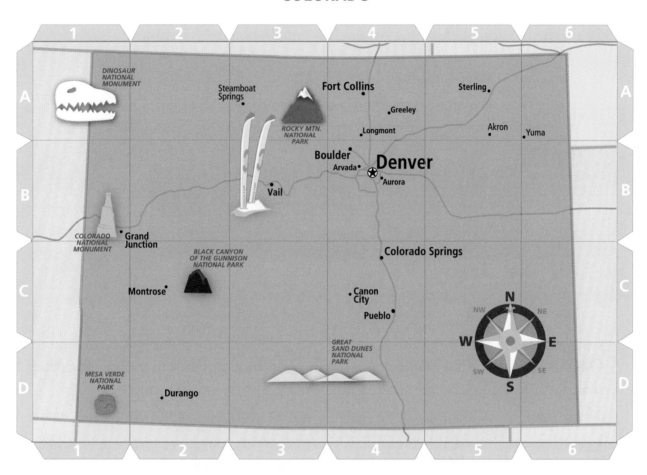

1. Start out in Colorado's capital and largest city in B4. What city is this?

   _____

2. Now it's time for fun on the slopes, and you're off to B3. What city are you in?

   _____

3. Then it's on to Dinosaur National Monument. Which square is it in? _____

4. Last stop—a national park in C2. What is its name?

   _____

Legend

⊛ Capital
● City
— Road

Map scales tell you how big the areas on a map really are. They show how distance on a map compares to the actual distance on Earth.

The most common way to show map scale is with a bar scale. A bar scale shows how inches (or centimeters) on a map are equal to miles (or kilometers) on land. You can see on the bar scale below that one inch is equal about to 230 miles.

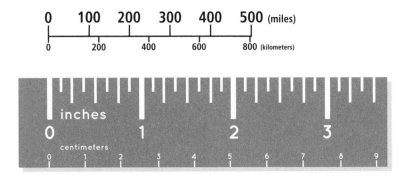

Copy the bar scale above onto a strip of paper. How many miles is it from Santa Fe to Oklahoma City on the map below? To find out, line up the 0 mark on your paper bar scale with Santa Fe and see where Oklahoma City falls on the scale.

How many miles is it from here to there in Ridgeland County? Copy the map scale below onto a strip of paper. Use your paper map scale and follow the roads to answer the questions.

RIDGELAND COUNTY

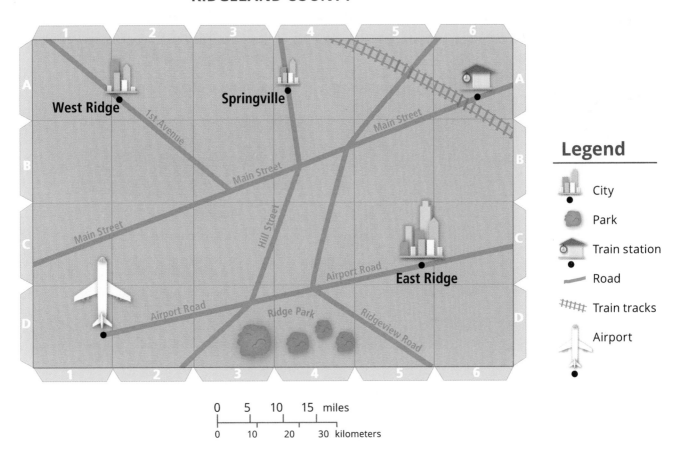

1. The distance from Springville to the corner of Hill Street and Main Street is about _____ miles or _____ kilometers.

2. East Ridge is about _____ miles or _____ kilometers from the airport.

3. True or false: If you follow the roads shown on the map, West Ridge is about 100 miles (about 160 kilometers) from Springville. _____

4. Which city is closest by road to the train station? _____

5. Which city is farthest by road from the airport? _____

6. You are at the corner of Ridgeview Road and Airport Road. You decide to travel north on Ridgeview Road. About how many miles or how many kilometers will you drive before you cross Main Street? _____

A **globe** is a model of the earth. It is shaped like a sphere, or ball, just like the earth. To see the entire earth, you have to spin the globe. A map of the earth is flat. It can show you all of the earth's surface at once. But how can you show the round earth on a flat map? It isn't easy!

There are different ways that people have figured out how to show the entire earth on a map, and these are called **projections**. There are two different map projections shown below.

ROBINSON PROJECTION OF THE EARTH

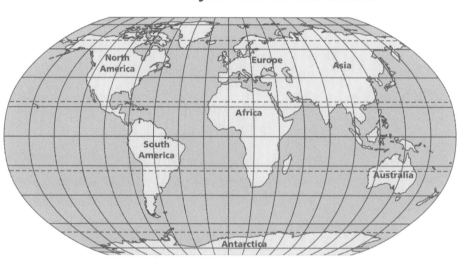

MILLER PROJECTION OF THE EARTH

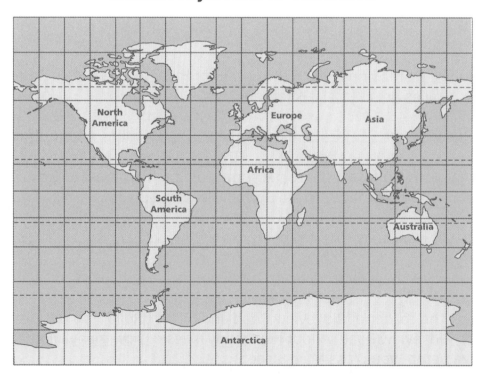

It's time for a little projection detection! Different projections use different methods to project the round earth onto a flat map. Can you spot differences between the two map projections on the opposite page? Write down at least four differences.

Projection Detection Differences

_____

_____

_____

_____

_____

Who Knew?

Smile for the Camera
Satellites are objects that orbit the earth and do things like take pictures from space. These pictures show lakes, rivers, roads, mountains—you name it! Satellites help mapmakers map places more accurately.

Some maps focus on one topic, or theme. These are called **thematic maps**. Thematic maps show lots of detail about a specific topic. There are many thematic map topics, such as physical features, population, climate, and environment. The thematic map on this page shows the yearly apple harvest of the area shown on the map.

YEARLY APPLE HARVEST MAP

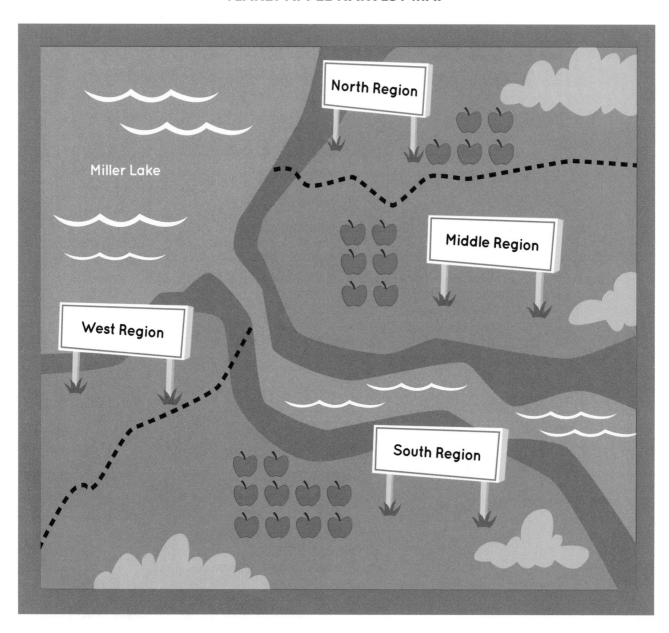

Legend

 = 1,000 bushels

It's time for you to take a bite out of a thematic map. Use the map and legend on the opposite page to answer the questions below

1. How many bushels does one apple represent on the map?

   _____

2. On the map, draw symbols to show that the West Region harvested 2,000 bushels.

3. How many bushels did the South Region harvest?

   _____

4. How many bushels did all the regions together harvest?

   _____

5. What symbol could you use to show 500 bushels?

   _____

A **physical map** is a thematic map that shows the physical, or natural, features of Earth. Physical features include major landforms such as mountains, hills, valleys, plains, and deserts. Physical maps also show oceans, lakes, and rivers.

Physical maps may include country borders and boundaries as well as cities and towns. Some physical maps offer elevations and depths. Elevations and depths tell how high the mountains and hills are and how deep the oceans and lakes are.

SOUTH AMERICA

Legend

- ⬤ Plains
- ⬤ Hills
- ⬤ Mountains
- ~ River

Unscramble the letters below to form words about physical maps. Then unscramble the circled letters to answer the questions.

1. This land is very dry.

T R(E)S(E)D _____
    1   2

2. Mountains and valleys are two types of these.

S M A N D(F)L(O)R _____
           3 4

3. Going up!

(E)L E V A N I O(T) _____
 5   6

4. This is flat land.

(S)P(L)A I(N) _____
 7 8   9

5. Another name for a border

N A R(Y)B O(U)D_____
      10   11

6. The exact ____ of a mountain is its elevation.

H G(H)T(E)I _____
     12 13

7. Water, water everywhere!

O(E)A N(C)_____
   14   15

8. Physical, or ____ features

(N)(A)A T R U L _____
 16 17

What does a physical map show?

____ ____ ____ ____ ____ ____ ____ ____
 8   12 10   7   9   15 16   4

____ ____ ____ ____ ____ ____ ____ ____
 3 13 17   6 11   1   5   2

Who Knew?

Machu Picchu
Can you imagine finding a city that no one knew existed?
That's what Hiram Bingham did. In 1911 he discovered the abandoned ruins of Machu Picchu, an ancient Incan city. There are many mysteries surrounding this city, including when and why it was abandoned.

A **political map** uses different colors to show the boundaries of continents, countries, states, provinces, or other territories.

The main purpose of a political map is to show human-made territory borders. Besides borders, a political map might also include features such as cities and towns. Some political maps show mountains, rivers and lakes, or other physical features. Those maps are called physical-political maps.

SOUTH AMERICA

Legend

* ✪ Capital
* ● City
* — Country boundary

Circle words about South America in the puzzle below.

Colombia
boundary
continent
country
ocean
sea
Peru
Brazil

O	C	E	A	N	C	N	B	C
B	T	E	P	M	O	D	A	O
O	X	A	V	B	L	L	I	U
U	K	J	S	T	O	E	L	N
N	O	W	E	M	M	G	I	T
D	F	O	A	K	B	H	Z	R
A	P	E	R	U	I	N	A	Y
R	E	D	R	O	A	L	R	C
Y	S	T	Q	A	A	Z	B	A
T	N	E	N	I	T	N	O	C

A **population map** is a kind of thematic map. It shows how many people live in the areas shown on the map.

Today the world has more than seven billion people. But the population is not evenly spread across all seven continents. More than half of the world's people live in Asia, and nobody lives permanently in Antarctica.

The map below shows which parts of the United States are most crowded and least crowded.

UNITED STATES: POPULATION

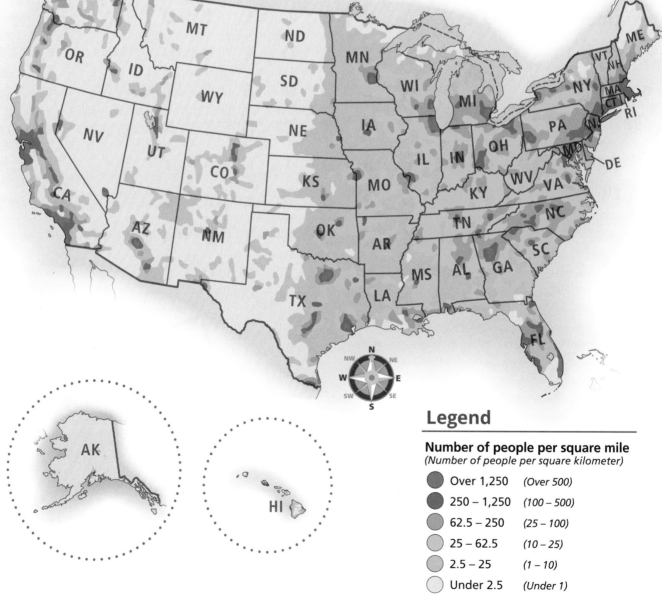

Legend

Number of people per square mile
(Number of people per square kilometer)

Over 1,250	*(Over 500)*
250 – 1,250	*(100 – 500)*
62.5 – 250	*(25 – 100)*
25 – 62.5	*(10 – 25)*
2.5 – 25	*(1 – 10)*
Under 2.5	*(Under 1)*

Use the population map on the opposite page to circle the right answers below. (If you need help with state abbreviations, see page 126.)

1. Which area of the U.S. has more people?   **East** or **West**

2. Which state has more people?   **Wyoming** or **Texas**

3. Which state has fewer people?   **Nevada** or **California**

4. Which state has more people?   **Hawaii** or **Alaska**

If you live in the United States, find your state on the map. Then look at the states that border your state. Does your state have more or fewer people than its neighboring states? _____

Who Knew?

I Need Some Space!
In large cities such as Tokyo, Japan, the trains that get people to work every day are jam-packed. At busy rush-hour times in Tokyo, there's even a white-gloved person who is hired to help gently push people into the trains.

A **climate map** is a thematic map that shows an area's average weather conditions. Temperature and precipitation (rain, snow, sleet, and hail) help form an area's climate.

Below is a climate map of Africa. Is most of Africa's desert in the northern or southern part of the continent?

AFRICA: CLIMATE

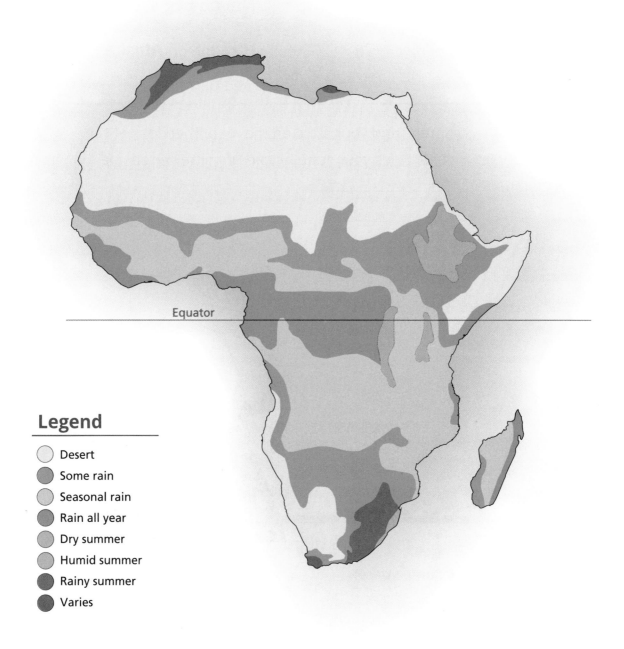

Equator

Legend

- Desert
- Some rain
- Seasonal rain
- Rain all year
- Dry summer
- Humid summer
- Rainy summer
- Varies

Are you cold or hot on climate? Find out by matching the terms below to their definitions. Use the information on the opposite page and in the "Who Knew?" box below to help you.

climate   equator   desert   precipitation   climate map

1. This kind of area is dry and gets very little precipitation. _____

2. Rain, snow, sleet, and hail _____

3. Temperatures are warmer the closer an area is to this ._____

4. A thematic map that shows an area's average weather conditions

    _____

5. An area's average weather conditions

    _____

Who Knew?

You're Getting Warmer!
Two important factors affect an area's climate. The first is distance from the equator —the closer an area is to the equator, the hotter its temperature will be throughout the year. The second factor is distance from the ocean. Areas near the ocean usually have less drastic swings in temperature from season to season.

A **land use map** is a special kind of thematic map that shows how people use an area of land. A land use map may also show physical features, such as lakes and mountains, or political features, such as country borders.

Land use maps are important because they show how people are affected by an area's physical features, climate, and natural resources. Below is a land use map of Australia. How do the people in most of the cities on the map use the land?

AUSTRALIA: LAND USE

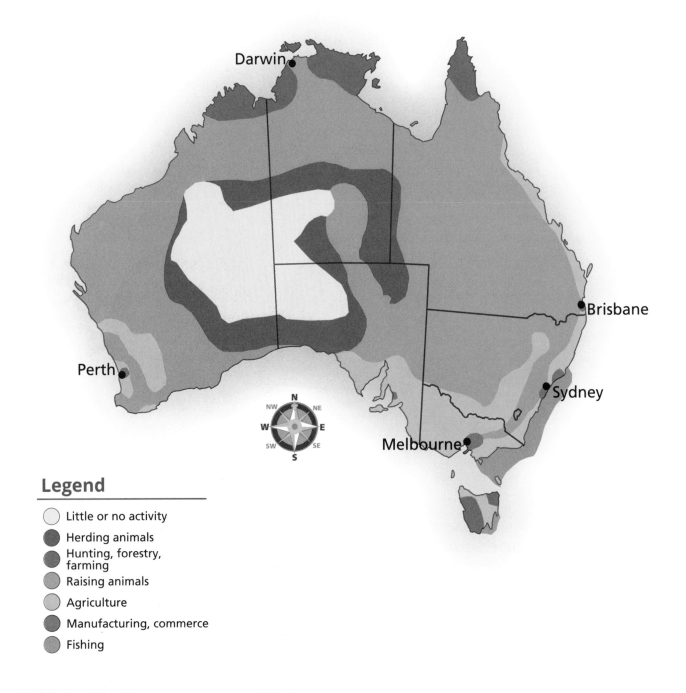

Legend

- ⬤ Little or no activity
- ⬤ Herding animals
- ⬤ Hunting, forestry, farming
- ⬤ Raising animals
- ⬤ Agriculture
- ⬤ Manufacturing, commerce
- ⬤ Fishing

Read the statements below and cross out the ones that are false.

1. Land use maps show how people use land.

2. Land use maps show how many people live in an area.

3. One way people might use the land is for farming.

4. The land use map of Australia on the opposite page shows where people herd animals.

5. A large part of Australia is used for hunting and fishing.

6. People can look at land use maps to find roads and highways.

Who Knew?

Counting Sheep
One of the ways that Australians use their land is for raising sheep. Australia has many sheep farms and is the world's largest producer of wool. So just how many sheep are there in Australia? There are about 75 million sheep, or three sheep for every person, in Australia.

An **environment map** is a type of thematic map that shows the different environments of a region or area. Some types of environments are forests, swamps, deserts, and grasslands. These are natural environments. Other environments, such as urban areas, or large cities, are created by people.

The environment map below shows the different environments found in the United States. What color are the urban areas on the map? Where is most of the cropland in the United States? (For a list of states and their abbreviations, see page 126.)

UNITED STATES: ENVIRONMENTS

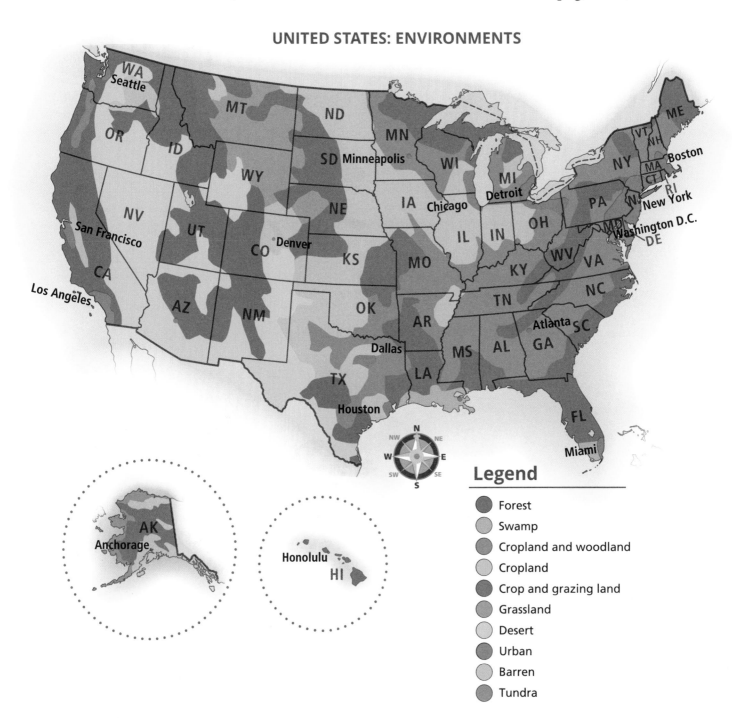

Legend

- Forest
- Swamp
- Cropland and woodland
- Cropland
- Crop and grazing land
- Grassland
- Desert
- Urban
- Barren
- Tundra

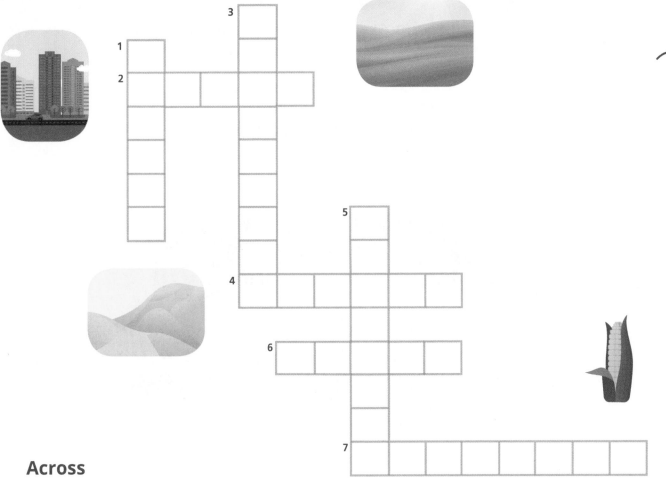

Across

2. Cities are _____ areas.

4. Almost all of Nevada has this type of environment.

6. You can find this type of wet land in Louisiana and Florida.

7. This is one kind of environment where you can grow food to eat.

Down

1. Part of Alaska's environment is called _____.

3. This environment is found in both Montana and Wyoming.

5. An environment map is a type of _____ map.

Who Knew?

Home Swampy Home
Florida's swamps are the home of both crocodiles and alligators. How do you tell them apart? Crocs are lighter in color and have longer, slimmer snouts. And when a croc's mouth is closed, you can still see its teeth.

Each half of Earth is called a **hemisphere**. Hemi- means "half," so a hemisphere is a "half sphere."

The equator is the line that divides Earth in half one way. All the land and water north of the equator is called the **Northern Hemisphere**, and all the land and water south of the equator is called the **Southern Hemisphere**.

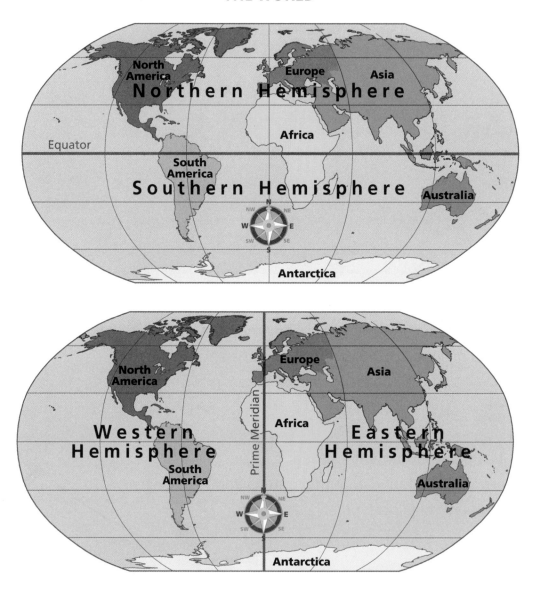

THE WORLD

There is another way to divide Earth in half. The **prime meridian** is the line that divides the earth in half the other way. All the land and water west of the prime meridian is called the **Western Hemisphere**, and all the land and water east of the prime meridian is called the **Eastern Hemisphere**.

Can you sort the continents into their hemispheres? Answer the questions in each of the hemisphere boxes.

Northern Hemisphere

1. Which two continents fall completely in the Northern Hemisphere?

_____

_____

Southern Hemisphere

2. Which two continents fall completely in the Southern Hemisphere?

_____

_____

Western Hemisphere

3. Which two continents fall completely in the Western Hemisphere?

_____

_____

Eastern Hemisphere

4. Which continent falls completely in the Eastern Hemisphere?

_____

5. Which other contents are mostly in the Eastern Hemisphere? (Look closely!)

_____

_____

_____

THE WORLD: CLIMATE

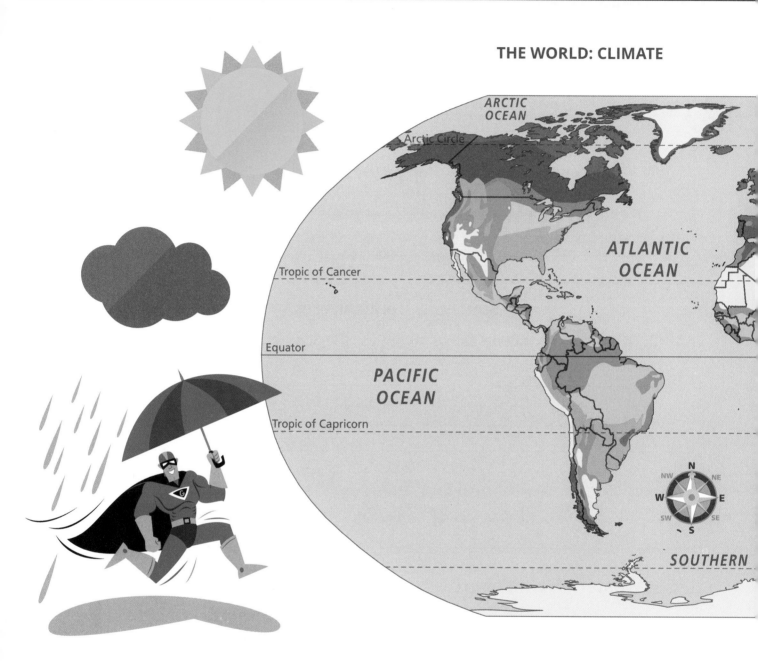

ARCTIC OCEAN

Arctic Circle

Tropic of Cancer

Equator

Tropic of Capricorn

PACIFIC OCEAN

ATLANTIC OCEAN

SOUTHERN

A world **climate map** shows the average daily weather conditions throughout the world.

Temperature and precipitation affect climate; so does the distance an area is from the equator. The closer a place is to the equator, the hotter it is. The hottest places in the world are those that fall between the latitude lines known as the Tropic of Cancer and the Tropic of Capricorn. (You will learn about latitude lines on page 34.) The farther a place is from the equator, the colder it is.

This map shows six climate types: tropical, dry, moderate, continental, polar, and highlands.

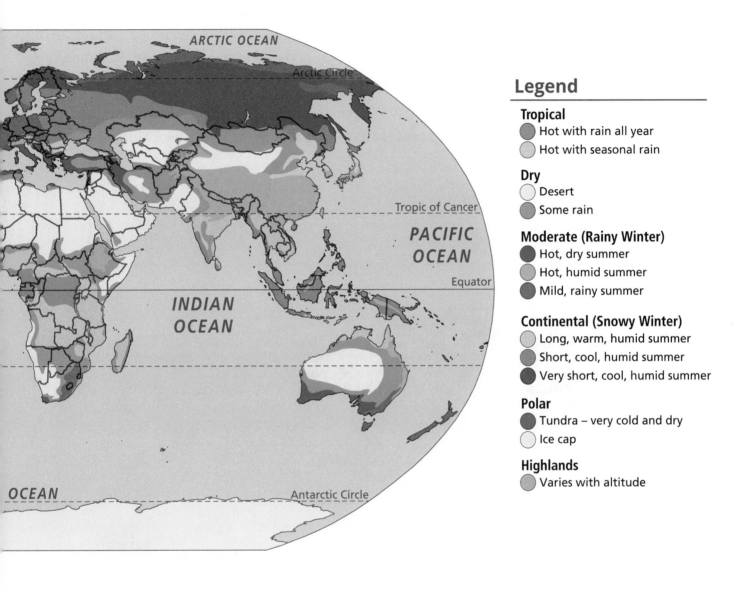

Legend

Tropical
- Hot with rain all year
- Hot with seasonal rain

Dry
- Desert
- Some rain

Moderate (Rainy Winter)
- Hot, dry summer
- Hot, humid summer
- Mild, rainy summer

Continental (Snowy Winter)
- Long, warm, humid summer
- Short, cool, humid summer
- Very short, cool, humid summer

Polar
- Tundra – very cold and dry
- Ice cap

Highlands
- Varies with altitude

Use the climate map and the legend to answer the questions.

1. Is a tropical climate hot or cold? _____

2. Circle three areas with a tropical climate on the map.

3. Circle the largest polar ice cap.

4. Is tundra rainy or dry? _____

5. Do dry climates ever have any rain? _____

6. Circle five dry climate areas on the map.

A **continent** is one of the world's seven large landmasses. The seven continents are North America, South America, Europe, Africa, Asia, Australia, and Antarctica. Asia and Europe share one continuous landmass. Sometimes they are combined and called Eurasia. Countries, islands, and other types of land make up a continent. Australia is the only continent that is also a country.

An ocean is a large body of water. Earth has five oceans: Pacific, Atlantic, Indian, Southern, and Arctic. These oceans surround the continents. Can you find all five oceans on the map?

THE WORLD

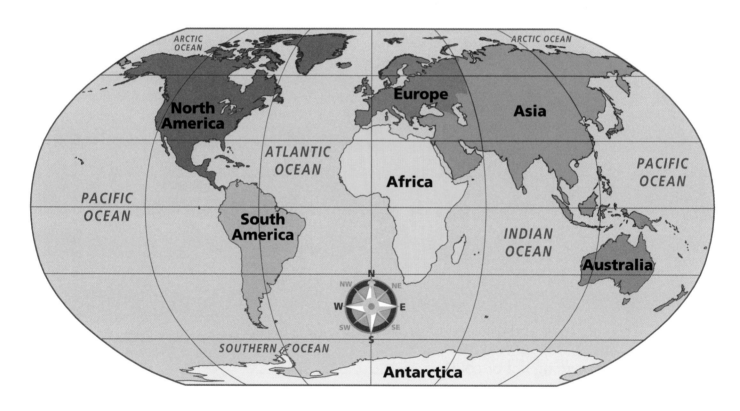

Draw lines to match the continents and oceans to their descriptions.

Arctic Ocean

Antarctica

South America

Indian Ocean

Asia

Australia

• The largest continent

• The smallest continent (It's also a country!)

• The northernmost ocean

• The southernmost continent (Penguins love it!)

• The continent south of North America

• One of the oceans that surrounds Africa

Who Knew?

The Blue Planet
Earth is sometimes called the "blue planet" because if you look at it from space, it's mostly blue. That's because about 75% of Earth's surface is covered by water.

Latitude and **longitude** are imaginary lines that circle the globe. Latitude lines run east and west, and longitude lines run north and south. The equator is a latitude line that divides the Northern Hemisphere from the Southern Hemisphere. The prime meridian is a longitude line that (along with the 180º line of longitude) divides the Eastern Hemisphere from the Western Hemisphere.

The lines of latitude and longitude are labeled with degrees. Both the equator and the prime meridian are labeled 0º. You can use the lines of latitude and longitude to find the location of places on Earth. Both the equator and the prime meridian run through one of the continents. Can you find which one?

THE WORLD

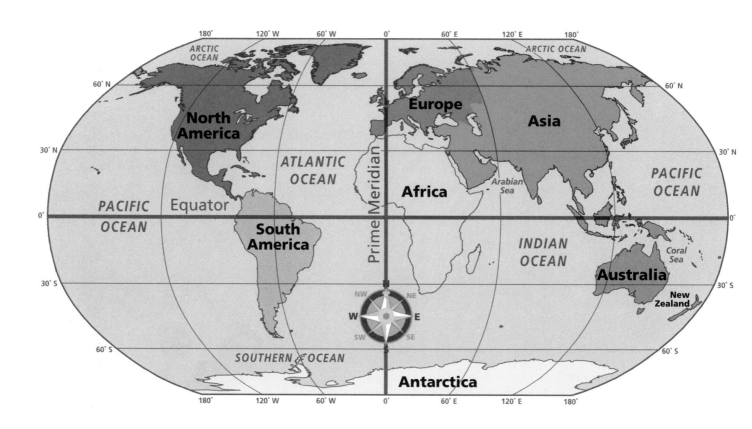

Use the latitude and longitude locations below to find your way around Africa. Fill in the name of the country at each location. Some of the letters have been filled in for you. Before you start, locate the equator and the prime meridian on the map below.

1. 15° S latitude and 45° E longitude   _____ a _____ a _____ a _____ _____ a _____

2. 15° N latitude and 30° E longitude   _____ _____ d _____ n

3. 30° N latitude and 15° E longitude   _____ i _____ _____ a

4. 30° N latitude and 0° longitude   _____ l _____ _____ r _____ _____

5. 0° latitude and 15° E longitude   _____ o _____ _____ o

AFRICA

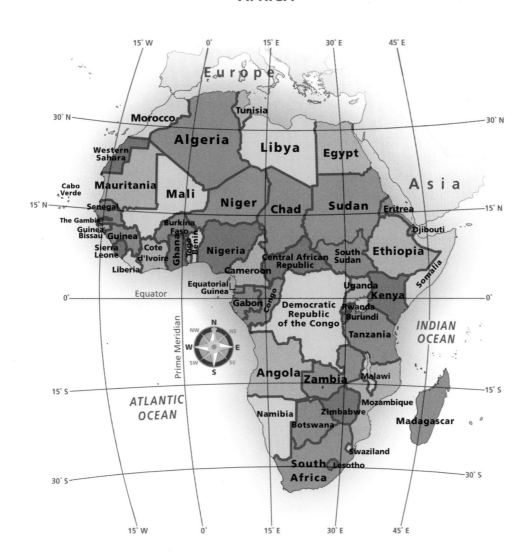

The world is divided into 24 **time zones**. You can figure out what time it is anywhere in the world by adding one hour for every time zone east of you and subtracting one hour for every time zone west of you.

The prime meridian, also called the Greenwich Meridian because it runs through Greenwich, England, is at 0° longitude. The time in Greenwich is called **Greenwich Mean Time** and is the standard of time used all over the world.

The international date line, also an imaginary line, is at 180° longitude. The time on both sides of the **international date line** is the same, but the day is not. West of the international date line, it is one day later than it is on the east side.

THE WORLD: TIME ZONES

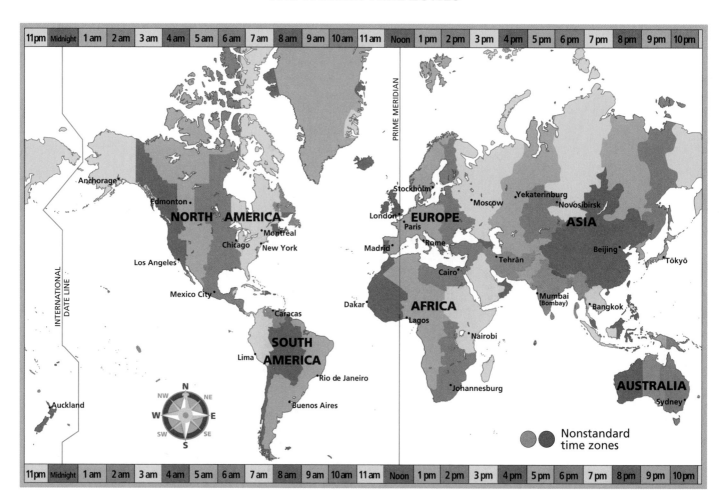

It's about time you learned about time! Use the time zone map to help you fill in the chart. Remember: as the time zones go from west to east, the time gets later by one hour for every zone.

What time is it here... ▶ ...if this is ▼ the time and date here?	New York, United States	Paris, France	Sydney, Australia
London, England 8:00 a.m. Thursday			
Mexico City, Mexico 5:00 p.m. Thursday			
Tokyo, Japan Midnight Thursday			

Who Knew?

Today or Tomorrow?
The tiny country of Kiribati, which is made up of many islands, used to be split by the international date line. In 1995, Kiribati officials "moved" the international date line to the east, so that all of the people on the islands would be west of the line and on the same day of the week.

North America is the third-largest continent and is made up of the Caribbean islands; the countries Canada, Mexico, and the United States; the seven countries of Central America (Belize, Costa Rica, El Salvador, Guatemala, Honduras, Nicaragua, and Panama); and the island of Greenland, which belongs to the country of Denmark in Europe. Greenland is the largest island in the world.

Three of the world's five oceans surround North America. They are the Pacific Ocean, the Atlantic Ocean, and the Arctic Ocean. Parts of Canada, the United States (Alaska), and Greenland (the world's largest island) lie within the Arctic Circle.

NORTH AMERICA

Do you know your continent? Study the map and information on the opposite page. Then read each sentence below and write a **T** if it is true and **F** if it is false. (No peeking!)

1. ____ The countries of Central America are part of North America.

2. ____ All of the world's five oceans surround North America.

3. ____ The Arctic Circle includes parts of Canada, Greenland, and the Caribbean Islands.

4. ____ Central America includes the countries of Costa Rica, Belize, and Alaska.

5. ____ North America is the largest continent.

6. ____ Greenland is the world's largest island.

Who Knew?

Walk from North America to Asia?
Before the earth's surface shifted thousands of years ago, North America and Asia were part of the same landmass. The land that is now Alaska was joined to what is now Russia. Today, the Bering Strait separates Asia from North America, where the two continents are fewer than 60 miles apart.

Canada is the largest country in North America and the second-largest country in the world (Russia is the largest). Much of Canada, however, is unpopulated because of its rugged land and very cold temperatures. Canada's people live mostly in the southern region closer to the United States border.

Canada has ten provinces and three territories. Can you find them on the map? In Ontario, Canada's largest province, are the country's capital city, Ottawa, and most populated city, Toronto.

CANADA

Legend

⊛ Country capital

● City

━ Country boundary

━ Province/Territory boundary

Unscramble the words to find the name of a Canadian province or territory. Then list the provinces or territories it borders.

Province/Territory	Bordering Provinces/Territories
Noyuk _____	_____ _____
Banamito _____	_____ _____ _____
Cebuqé _____	_____ _____ _____

Who Knew?

Giving Beavers a Break
Canada's national animal is the beaver. In the 1600s and 1700s, Europeans thought it was fashionable to wear hats made from beaver pelts. Canada's huge beaver population was almost wiped out by the demand. Fortunately for the beavers, the fashion changed to silk hats!

CANADA

United States

Yukon

Northwest Territories

British Columbia

Alberta

Manitoba

Saskatchewan

Nunavut

Iqaluit ★

Greenland (Denmark)

ATLANTIC OCEAN

Newfoundland and Labrador

N
NW   NE
W   E
SW   SE
S

PACIFIC OCEAN

Ontario

Québec

Prince Edward Island

New Brunswick

Nova Scotia

Québec ★

Montreal ●

United States

ATLANTIC OCEAN

Legend

★ Province capital
● City
— Country boundary
— Province boundary

Canadians speak many languages and come from different backgrounds. Canada's official languages are French and English. Most French-speaking Canadians live in the province of **Québec**. Montréal, the largest city in Québec, is the second-largest French-speaking city in the world.

Another group of people who live in Canada are the Inuit. They are a group of native people who make up nearly all of the population of **Nunavut**. The Inuit make use of the land by hunting animals such as seal and caribou for food, clothing, and trade. The Inuit speak a language called Inuktitut.

Use the map and the information on the opposite page to answer these questions about Québec and Nunavut.

1. What is the capital of Québec? _____

2. What is the capital of Nunavut? _____

3. What body of water separates western Québec from eastern Nunavut?

_____

4. What provinces or territories border Nunavut? _____

5. What languages are spoken in Québec? _____

Who Knew?

Pass the Syrup, Please
Maple syrup is made only in North America, and Québec is one of the leading makers. In spring, when the sap begins to rise in the maple trees, it is tapped, or collected, and then boiled for hours to make syrup. Pancakes, anyone?

The **United States** is the most populated country in North America. It's bordered by Canada to the north and Mexico to the south.

There are 50 states in the U.S., and the 48 contiguous, or joined, states are between two of the world's five oceans, the Pacific on the west and the Atlantic on the east. The nation's capital is Washington, D.C., and the three most populated cities are New York, Los Angeles, and Chicago. Do you know where these cities are located? Circle them on the map.

UNITED STATES

Legend

⊛ Country capital
● City
— Country boundary
— State boundary

Can you name the states? There are seven states that fit in the puzzle below. Use the letters that have been filled in to help you find the answers.

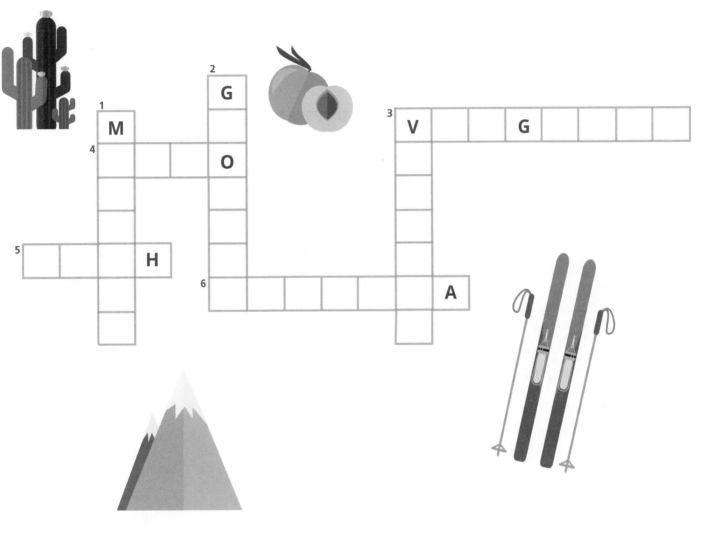

The United States of America is a large country with many people, cultures, and environments. The United States is often divided into different regions, and each region often has its own traditions and climate. One way of dividing the country is shown on the map below. The regions on this map are Northeast, Mid-Atlantic, Midwest, Great Plains, South, Southwest, Rocky Mountain, and Pacific.

UNITED STATES: REGIONS

What's in a name? The regions of the U.S. are named for different reasons. Fill in the region names in the boxes below.

Regions Named for Physical Features

_____   _____

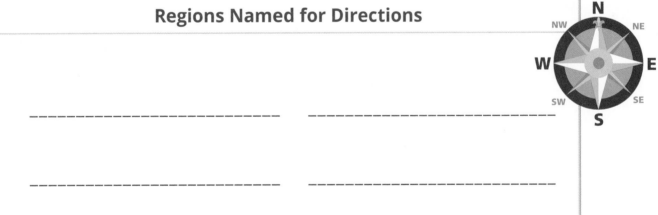

Regions Named for Oceans

_____   _____

Regions Named for Directions

_____   _____

_____   _____

Who Knew?

Drink Up
The United States has only one official language, English. But that doesn't mean everyone uses the same words. To many people in the Midwest, a soft drink is called "pop." To many others in the Mid-Atlantic and Northeast regions, it's "soda." And Southerners tend to call any soft drink "Coke™," regardless of the brand.

The **Northeast** and **Mid-Atlantic** regions are in the northeastern part of the United States. These regions border the Atlantic Ocean. Some people call a section of the Northeast region New England, which includes Connecticut, Maine, Massachusetts, New Hampshire, Rhode Island, and Vermont. Can you find these states on the map? (For a list of state abbreviations, see page 126.)

In these regions you'll find nine of the original 13 U.S. colonies. These colonies were started by Great Britain. In 1776, the colonies declared their independence and eventually formed the United States.

UNITED STATES: NORTHEAST AND MID-ATLANTIC REGIONS

Unscramble the names below to find out which nine states in this region were part of the original 13 colonies. Then place the circled letters in the blanks below to write the abbreviations of the other four states that made up the original colonies. One letter has been filled in for you.

1. NECNOTTUCIC _____
3

2. LARWADEE _____
7

3. DARYMANL _____

4. SAMSSETATSHUC _____
5

5. WESJYNEER _____
4

6. PHSIEREWNMAH _____

7. KORNWEY _____
2

8. HASIRDOLEND _____
1

9. NANNYVESPALI _____
6

G __ __   __ __ __   __ __   __ __
    1   2 3   4 5   6 7

Do you know the full state name for each of the four abbreviations? Write them here. Look at page 126 if you need help.

_____   _____

_____   _____

The **Midwest** and **Great Plains** regions are in the central part of the United States. These regions are known for their prairies and farmlands.

The Great Lakes and the Mississippi River have always been important waterways in these regions. The Great Lakes are so large that they are sometimes called "freshwater seas." And the Mississippi River is the largest river in the country.

UNITED STATES: GREAT PLAINS AND MIDWEST REGIONS

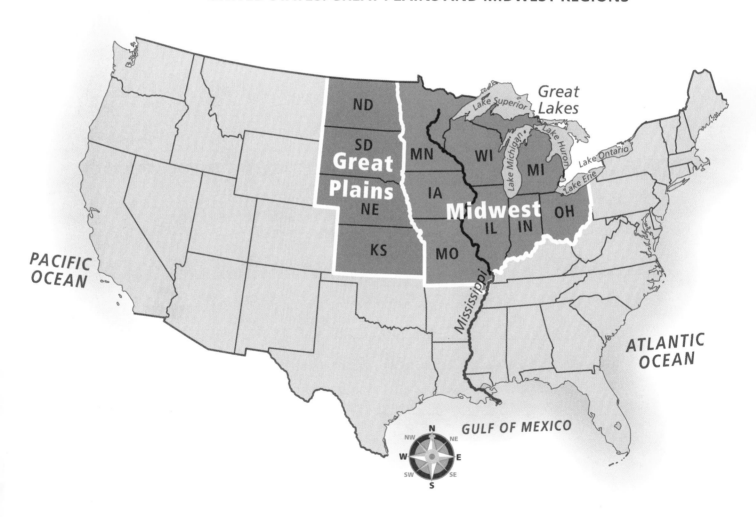

Ride the waves of the Great Lakes to solve the riddles below. Remember to look at page 126 if you need help with state abbreviations.

1. This state and lake name are one and the same. _____

2. This lake is not inferior; that's why we call it Lake _____

3. Travel from Ohio to the north and this lake will come forth. _____

Name the Midwestern states that border the Great Lakes.

_____

_____

_____

_____

_____

_____

Who Knew?

Great Glaciers
More than a million years ago, there were glaciers where the Great Lakes are now. These glaciers moved very slowly across the land. Then the glaciers melted over many, many years, creating the lakes.

The **South** and the **Southwest** regions are known for their hot climates, but the South tends to be humid while the Southwest is dry.

The South's warm weather and many beaches make it a popular destination for tourists. Many American music traditions, such as jazz, blues, country, and rock n' roll, got their start in the South.

The Southwest's warm, dry climate and fascinating landscape, which includes desert, canyons, and mountains, make it another popular tourist destination. You can find many Mexican cultural influences in the Southwest, since much of its land once belonged to Mexico.

If you need help with state abbreviations, see page 126.

UNITED STATES: SOUTH AND SOUTHWEST REGIONS

What's the same? What's different? Compare and contrast the South and Southwest. In each circle, write down the words or phrases that apply to that region. In the area where the circles overlap, write down the words or phrases that apply to both regions.

hot
humid
dry
canyons
popular with tourists
beaches
desert
some states border the ocean

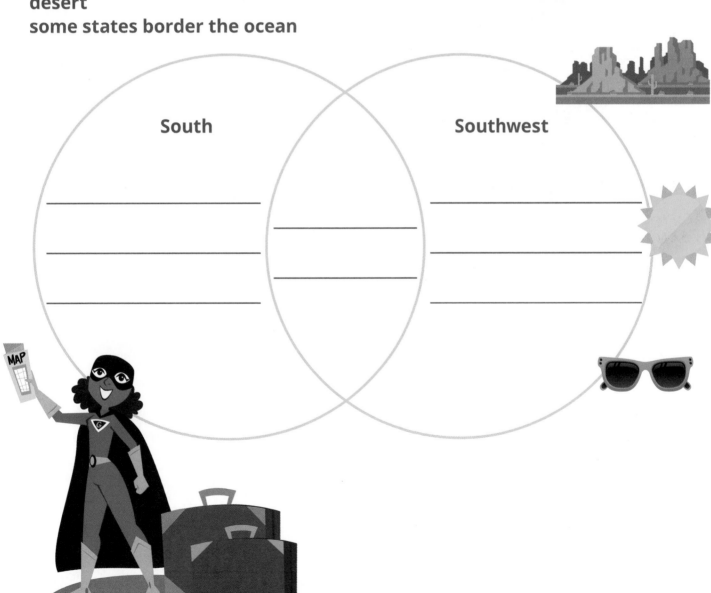

South

Southwest

When settlers from Europe first came to the United States, they came to the East. Over time, people moved to the open lands of the West. The **Rocky Mountain** region is known for its beautiful landscape: the Rocky Mountains and forested land. Logging is an important industry in this area. The **Pacific** region is well known for its long Pacific coastline and abundant fishing. Hawaii and Alaska are considered part of the Pacific region.

If you need help with state abbreviations, see page 126.

UNITED STATES: PACIFIC AND ROCKY MOUNTAIN REGIONS

The search is on! Circle these words about the Rocky Mountain and Pacific regions in the puzzle below.

West	mountains	coastline
fishing	forests	Wyoming
California	Colorado	logging

X	M	K	E	L	P	G	D	U	N	O	O	T
O	U	E	F	G	W	I	N	J	Q	N	Y	S
M	C	E	M	F	Y	A	U	I	R	J	N	Y
Q	O	D	A	R	O	L	O	C	H	M	J	A
L	A	L	E	C	M	R	Y	U	F	S	B	D
D	S	I	A	I	I	C	E	J	I	O	I	B
T	T	A	L	O	N	T	K	S	E	F	X	F
P	L	L	O	G	G	I	N	G	T	D	C	L
A	I	T	V	U	M	K	P	W	E	S	T	P
S	N	I	A	T	N	U	O	M	S	S	L	Z
F	E	C	A	L	I	F	O	R	N	I	A	N

The official name of **Mexico** is the United Mexican States. The official language is Spanish. The United States borders Mexico, and so do the countries Belize and Guatemala.

Mexico has 31 states and one federal district, which is the location of the capital city, Mexico City. Mexico City is not only one of the largest cities in the world, but it is also the oldest capital city in North or South America.

MEXICO

United States

Mexico

GULF OF MEXICO

PACIFIC OCEAN

Mexico City ✪

Belize

Guatemala

Legend

✪ Country capital
— Country boundary
— State boundary

Get to know Mexico. Fill in the answers as you work your way through the country. Use the information and the map on the opposite page to help you.

1. What is Mexico's official name?

_____

2. What language is spoken in Mexico?

_____

3. What is the capital city?

_____

4. What countries border Mexico?

_____

5. How many states does Mexico have?

_____

6. What ocean borders Mexico on the west?

_____

Who Knew?

Sugary, Not Scary
Every year in November, Mexicans celebrate a holiday known as Dia de los Muertos, or Day of the Dead. It isn't a scary day like Halloween, though. It's a time to remember loved ones who have died. Families celebrate by putting up photographs of the person who has passed away. Many people also celebrate by eating sugar candy in the shape of skulls!

Mexico has many industries, such as oil, silver mining, and farming. Many farms are in the north of the country. They grow corn, oranges, apples, grapes, and other fruits and vegetables.

Tourism is also important to Mexico. The cities of Acapulco, Ixtapa, and Cancun are popular areas where visitors can swim, enjoy the sunshine, and fish.

Mexico City has many of the country's important government offices and big businesses. It also has more than 100,000 factories!

MEXICO

United States

GULF OF CALIFORNIA

Mexico

GULF OF MEXICO

PACIFIC OCEAN

Cancun

Mexico City ✹

Ixtapa

Acapulco

Belize

Guatemala

N NE
NW
W E
SW SE
S

Legend

✹ Capital
● City
— Country boundary

Complete the puzzle with what you have learned about Mexico.

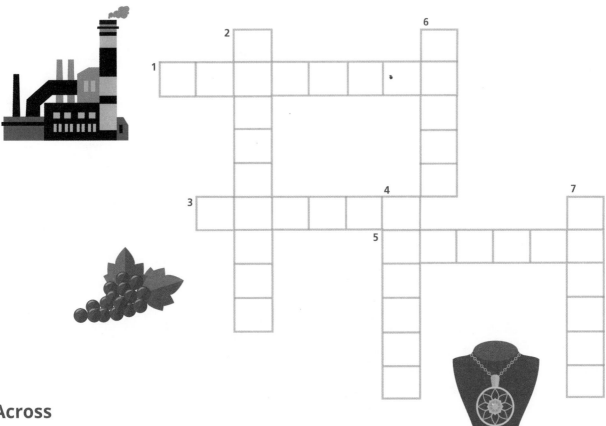

Across

1. A tourist city on the Pacific coast

3. One of many fruits grown in Mexico

5. Another tourist city

Down

2. You'll find lots of these in Mexico City

4. A shiny ore mined in Mexico

6. Many Mexican farms are located in the _____.

7. A city on the Gulf of Mexico

Who Knew?

Gracias for Chocolate

Did you know that we have Mexico to thank for chocolate? Long ago in Mexico, people called Aztecs made a drink from cacao beans, vanilla, spices, and water. They called this drink *xocoatl* (pronounced show-coat-el), or bitter water. If you've ever tried unsweetened chocolate, you know why. What word does "xocoatl" remind you of?

Middle America is a region that includes the Caribbean islands and the countries south of Mexico and north of Colombia. Part of the Middle America region includes the countries of Central America: Guatemala, Belize, El Salvador, Honduras, Nicaragua, Costa Rica, and Panama. Central America's beautiful land is also home to earthquakes, especially along the west coast. Central America's land is ideal for growing coffee, bananas, sugarcane, and other crops.

MIDDLE AMERICA

Legend

— Country boundary

United States

GULF OF MEXICO

Miami

Bahamas

ATLANTIC OCEAN

Cuba

Turks and Caicos Islands (U.K.)

Mexico

Cayman Islands (U.K.)

Belize

Haiti

Dominican Republic

British Virgin Islands

Virgin Islands (U.S.)

Anguilla (U.K.)

Sint Maarten (Neth.)

Guatemala

Jamaica

Puerto Rico (U.S.)

Saint Kitts and Nevis

Antigua and Barbuda

Honduras

Montserrat (U.K.)

Guadeloupe (Fr.)

El Salvador

CARIBBEAN SEA

Dominica

Martinique (Fr.)

Nicaragua

Saint Lucia

Saint Vincent and the Grenadines

Barbados

Aruba (Neth.)

Curaçao (Neth.)

Grenada

Costa Rica

Trinidad and Tobago

Panama

Venezuela

Colombia

Look at the map on the opposite page and answer the questions to test your knowledge of Middle America.

1. These two Central American countries border Mexico.

_____   _____

2. This country borders Colombia, a country in South America.

_____

3. Which two countries border Nicaragua?

_____   _____

4. Which country borders Honduras and Guatemala?

_____

5. What group of islands is nearest to the U.S. city of Miami?

_____

6. What do the countries of Haiti and the Dominican Republic share?

_____

Who Knew?

Memory Helper
Need help remembering the countries of Central America from north to south? Think of this sentence to remember the first letter in each country's name:
Great Big Eaters Have Nice Clean Plates.

Middle America includes the **Caribbean islands**. Different languages are spoken on the islands. Depending on the island, the language could be French, Spanish, English, or something else. Hundreds of years ago, the European explorer Christopher Columbus landed in the Caribbean—but he thought he was in Asia instead!

CARIBBEAN ISLANDS

United States

GULF OF MEXICO

Bahamas

Nassau ⊛

Havana ⊛

Cuba

Turks and Caicos Islands (U.K.)

Mexico

Cayman Islands (U.K.)

Haiti

Dominican Republic

Jamaica

Port-au-Prince ⊛

Santo Domingo ⊛

Belize

⊛ Kingston

Honduras

CARIBBEAN SEA

N
NW NE
W E
SW SE
S

Nicaragua

Curaçao (Neth.)

Aruba (Neth.)

Costa Rica

Panama

South

Legend

⊛ Country capital

— Country boundary

Hop around the Caribbean by matching each island below to its capital city.

Port-au-Prince

Nassau

Havana

Kingston

San Juan

Santa Domingo

1. Cuba

✷ _____

2. Puerto Rico

✷ _____

3. Dominican Republic

✷ _____

4. Haiti

✷ _____

5. Jamaica

✷ _____

6. Bahamas

✷ _____

ATLANTIC
OCEAN

British
Virgin
Islands
Virgin Islands (U.K.) Anguilla
Islands (U.K.) (U.K.)
(U.S.)

San Juan

Sint Maarten (Neth.)

Puerto
Rico
(U.S.)

Basseterre
Saint Kitts
and Nevis

Antigua and Barbuda

Saint John's

Montserrat
(U.K.)

Guadeloupe
(Fr.)

Dominica

Roseau

Martinique
(Fr.)

Castries Saint Lucia

Saint Vincent and
the Grenadines Kingstown

Bridgetown
Barbados

Grenada

Saint George's

Trinidad and
Tobago

Port of Spain

America

The continent of **South America** is known for having some of the most diverse landscape in the world. South America has the Andes Mountains that run north to south along the western coast, the Amazon rain forest in northern Brazil, and the grassy regions of northern Argentina and Uruguay.

Most of South America's people live in cities near the coast. That's why this is sometimes called the "hollow continent."

SOUTH AMERICA

Venezuela

Guyana
Suriname
French Guiana

Colombia

ATLANTIC OCEAN

Ecuador

Amazon Amazon

Peru

Rain Forest

Andes Mountains

Brazil

Bolivia

PACIFIC OCEAN Chile

Paraguay

N
NW NE
W E
SW SE
S

Uruguay

Argentina

ATLANTIC OCEAN

Falkland Islands

Legend

● Plains
● Hills
● Mountains
⌒ River

Get to know the countries of South America and where they are located. Use the physical map on the opposite page to help you find the countries, then label them on the political map of South America on this page. The country names are listed below. Can you do it without peeking at the opposite page?

Argentina

Bolivia

Brazil

Chile

Colombia

Ecuador

Falkland Islands

French Guiana

Guyana

Paraguay

Peru

Suriname

Uruguay

Venezuela

Who Knew?

Bring an Umbrella!
The Amazon rain forest gets more than 100 inches (254 centimeters) of rain a year. It is the largest tropical rain forest in the world, spreading across 1.2 billion acres and nine countries.

100"

What do **llamas** and **anacondas** have in common? Both live in South America—llamas in the Andes Mountains and anacondas in the shallow waters of the Amazon River Basin.

Llamas are pack animals that help people carry things. They have thick woolly coats to keep them warm and are very good at climbing high in the mountains.

The anaconda is a reptile. It is one of the world's largest snakes. Some anacondas grow to more than 30 feet (about 9 meters) long. They are more at home in shallow water than on land, but they can climb trees really well.

Who Knew?

Spitting Mad!
Llamas are usually calm and gentle, but they do spit at each other during arguments over food or to establish who's boss. Maybe that's where the phrase "spitting mad" comes from!

Would you rather climb a mountain or slither through a river basin? Choose one of the activities below, and get a friend to do the other one. Start at the bottom, and see who finishes first!

Ready... Set... Go!

3. Why are llamas suited to cold mountain air?

_____

_____

2. Which South American mountain range do llamas live in?

_____

1. True or False: Llamas are good at climbing trees.

_____

3. If you want to find an anaconda in South America, which river basin should you look in?

_____

2. Do anacondas like deep water or shallow water?

_____

1. True or False: You'd be more likely to find an anaconda on the ground than in the water.

_____

BEST TIME:

_____min. _____sec.

BEST TIME:

_____min. _____sec.

South American farmers grow many types of foods such as coffee and sugarcane. Much of the farming is done in the flat, level plains.

Almost half of the world's coffee comes from South America. Other important crops are bananas, oranges, and cocoa. Look on the map to see where the different crops grow. Which one would you like to snack on?

SOUTH AMERICA: PRODUCTS

Legend

- Coffee
- Sugarcane
- Bananas
- Cocoa
- Oranges

You are planning to import coffee beans, sugarcane, oranges, and bananas from South America, but you're not sure how much of each item to buy. Use the legend and the hints below to figure it out.

 = 5 pounds bananas   = 10 pounds sugarcane

 = 20 pounds oranges   = 50 pounds coffee beans

1. x = _____ pounds of bananas

2. + + = _____ pounds of oranges and

_____ pounds of bananas

3. + − + = _____ pounds of coffee beans and

_____ pounds of oranges

4. x x = _____ pounds of sugarcane

A **rain forest** is a dense forest that gets at least 100 inches (254 centimeters) of rain a year. The Amazon rain forest in South America has more species of plants and animals than any other place in the world!

This is where you can find beautiful flowers like orchids and lilies, green plants such as ferns, and fungi such as mushrooms. You might also see animals such as tree-dwelling sloths, turtles, frogs, pig-like tapirs, and brightly colored toucan birds.

SOUTH AMERICA: AMAZON RAIN FOREST

Amazon
Rain Forest

Atacama Desert

Legend

- Rain forest
- Country boundary

Circle the names of these rain forest plants and animals in the puzzle below.

sloth
turtles
tapir
toucan
frogs
orchids
ferns
fungi
lilies

F	R	T	L	O	A	E	I	M	J
M	R	C	E	T	A	I	N	X	L
N	I	O	H	R	A	L	S	V	L
O	P	R	G	E	M	I	C	U	T
P	A	I	G	S	L	L	O	L	O
R	T	F	U	N	G	I	A	N	E
T	T	E	B	K	I	E	L	A	A
U	U	R	I	L	S	S	R	C	B
V	R	N	S	L	O	T	H	U	O
W	T	S	D	I	H	C	R	O	T
X	L	S	C	I	A	L	O	T	L
L	E	J	E	E	U	I	L	P	B
T	S	A	N	B	J	O	D	Q	J

Who Knew?

Thirsty?
Chile is home to one of the driest places on Earth—the Atacama Desert. In parts of this desert, no rainfall has ever been recorded!

The continent of South America has several active **volcanoes**. Many of them are in the Andes Mountains in the countries of Chile, Ecuador, and Colombia. Villarrica is considered one of Chile's most active volcanoes. Colombia's highest active volcano is called Huila. Cotopaxi in Ecuador is the world's highest active volcano. Can you find other volcanoes on the map?

SOUTH AMERICA: VOLCANOES

Legend

▲ Volcano
— Country boundary

Match the names of the volcanoes to the countries where they're located.

Villarrica   Cotopaxi   Copahue

Sangay   Huila   Cerro Azul

Sumaco   Tolima   Galeras

| Ecuador | Chile | Columbia |

The continent of Europe is smaller than all the other continents except Australia. Seven countries in Europe are even smaller than the U.S. state of Rhode Island. These countries are Vatican City, Monaco, San Marino, Liechtenstein, Malta, Andorra, and Luxembourg. Can you find them on the map?

Even though it is small, Europe is very densely populated. It has more people than any continent except Asia and Africa.

EUROPE

Legend

— Country boundary

Who am I? Read each clue and write the name of the country on the line.

1. I am south of France and east of Portugal. _____

2. Part of my land is in southeastern Europe, but most of me is in Asia.

   _____

3. I border Russia, Moldova, and five other countries, and my name starts and ends with a vowel.

   _____

4. I am one of the northernmost countries in Europe, and I am also an island.

   _____

5. You can find me between Norway and Finland.

   _____

Who Knew?

A Quick Stroll Around the Country
At less than one square mile each, Vatican City and Monaco are the two smallest countries in the world.

Water, Water Everywhere!

Before there were cars or airplanes, **rivers** gave people an easy way to travel long distances. Many important cities grew around rivers, such as London around the Thames and Paris around the Seine.

Other bodies of water, such as **lakes** and **seas**, are also important. Some of the seas that surround Europe help link it to other continents.

EUROPE: WATERWAYS

Legend

~ River

● City

— Country boundary

You are a tour guide planning a trip on Europe's seas. Complete the chart for your travelers. What seas or channels will you cross on your trip from city to city?

On our trip, we will travel these waterways:

FROM	TO	SEAS OR CHANNELS
London	Paris	_____
Rome	Madrid	_____
Venice	Athens	_____
Dublin	London	_____

Who Knew?

Help, I'm Sinking!
To get around the city of Venice—a city built on water—people use boats or gondolas. It's a good thing, too, because Venice is sinking! It's not by much, but each year the city sinks a little bit more into the sea.

Skiing. Hiking. Climbing. These are just some of the activities you can do in the mountains. Europe has many mountain ranges. Some ranges are more well-known than others, like the Alps, and some are smaller than others, like the Carpathian Mountains.

Mountains have also helped shape country borders. For example, the Pyrenees separate France and Spain. The Ural Mountains in Russia help form a natural boundary that separates the continents of Europe and Asia.

EUROPE: MOUNTAIN RANGES

Climb to the top of the mountain by unscrambling the letters to form the names of European mountain ranges.

7. **laur**

_____

6. **caanathirp**

_____

5. **ccaauuss**

_____

4. **apensenin**

_____

3. **penserye**

_____

2. **caananbrit**

_____

1. **pals**

_____

Europe has many landmarks that were built a long time ago. Some of these landmarks are very old, such as Stonehenge in England, the Parthenon in Greece, and the Colosseum in Italy. Europe also has many old castles that once offered protection from enemies and invaders. Some landmarks, like the Eiffel Tower in France, were built more recently.

Stonehenge

This landmark is a monument made of enormous stones standing in a circle. It was built about 5,000 years ago.

Windmills

In the Netherlands, windmills were built to harness the power of the wind to do things like grind grain or pump water. These days, they can even use the wind to generate electricity.

Colosseum

Ancient Romans flocked to this enormous building to watch professional fighters known as gladiators. It's now in ruins, but it used to be much like a modern sports arena.

Castles

Early castles were built mostly to serve as fortresses against enemies. Later, castles were built as beautiful, elaborate places to live. In Germany, many castles were built near the Rhine River.

Parthenon

The Parthenon stands atop a plateau in Greece known as the Acropolis. It was both a temple and a treasury for the ancient Greeks.

Eiffel Tower

The Eiffel Tower was built in Paris, France in 1889 for a world's fair. At the time, it was the tallest building in the world.

How well do you know Europe's landmarks? Use this crossword puzzle to find out.

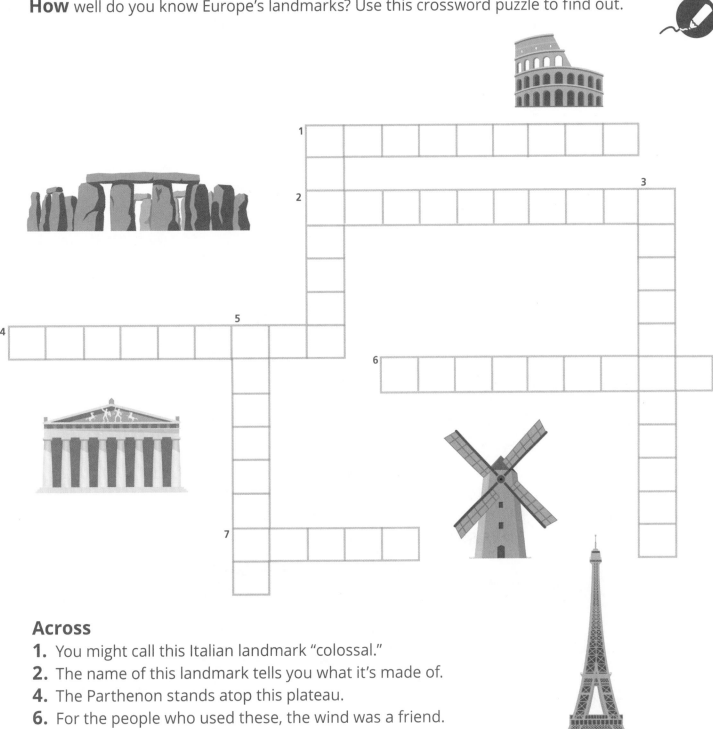

Across

1. You might call this Italian landmark "colossal."
2. The name of this landmark tells you what it's made of.
4. The Parthenon stands atop this plateau.
6. For the people who used these, the wind was a friend.
7. Many castles are located on this German river.

Down

1. These once offered protection from invaders.
3. This was built for a world's fair.
5. The ancient monument of Stonehenge is one of these.

Much of the land in Europe is used for farming, and each country is known for its own foods. One food many European countries make is cheese, which is made from the milk of cows, goats, and even sheep.

If you like pizza, you can thank Italy, where mozzarella comes from. Brie from France is delicious with crusty bread and a bit of jam. Greece and other countries make salty feta from goat's milk. And Limburger from Germany is tasty but stinky. Do you think that gouda from the Netherlands is "gouda" for you?

EUROPE: CHEESES

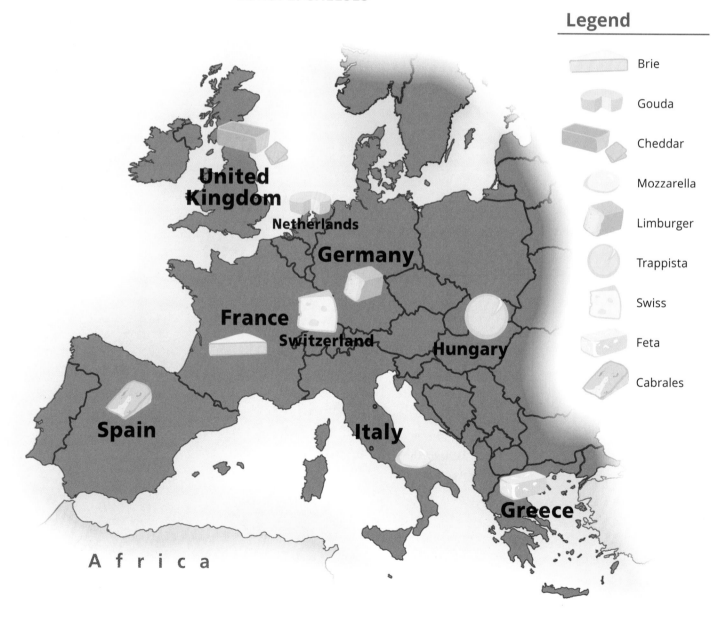

Legend

- Brie
- Gouda
- Cheddar
- Mozzarella
- Limburger
- Trappista
- Swiss
- Feta
- Cabrales

Imagine you are traveling all around Europe, eating cheese in each country you stop in along the way. In your travel journal, write down the names of the countries and the name of the cheese you tasted in each one.

TRAVEL JOURNAL

Country	Cheese
_____	_____
_____	_____
_____	_____
_____	_____
_____	_____
_____	_____
_____	_____
_____	_____
_____	_____

Africa is bordered by the Atlantic Ocean on the west and the Indian Ocean on the east. It is separated from Europe and Asia by the Mediterranean and Red Seas.

Sometimes people mistakenly think that Africa is a country. Actually, it's a continent made up of 58 countries. People also sometimes assume that the continent is one big desert. While much of Africa's land is desert, it also has other environments, such as forest.

AFRICA

Legend

— Country boundary

The names of African countries start with many different letters of the alphabet. Fill in the missing country names to spell the phrase "African continent" without writing the same country name twice.

A _ _ _ _ _ _ _

SOUTH A**F**RICA

R _ _ _ _ _ _

ZA**I**RE

C _ _ _ _

A _ _ _ _ _ _

NIGER

C _ _ _ _ _

MOR**O**CCO

N _ _ _ _ _ _ _

T _ _ _ _

LIBER**I**A

N _ _ _ _ _ _

E _ _ _ _

SE**N**EGAL

T _ _ _ _ _ _

MAP MIXER

Africa has more countries than any other continent. The map on the left shows you that about 55 years ago, countries in Europe, such as Britain and France, controlled all but four countries in Africa. What does the map on the right show you?

There are more than 800 languages spoken in Africa. Each country has at least one official language, but many different tribes and groups still speak their own languages. One language many Africans speak is Swahili. *Unazungumza Kiswahili?* (Do you speak Swahili?)

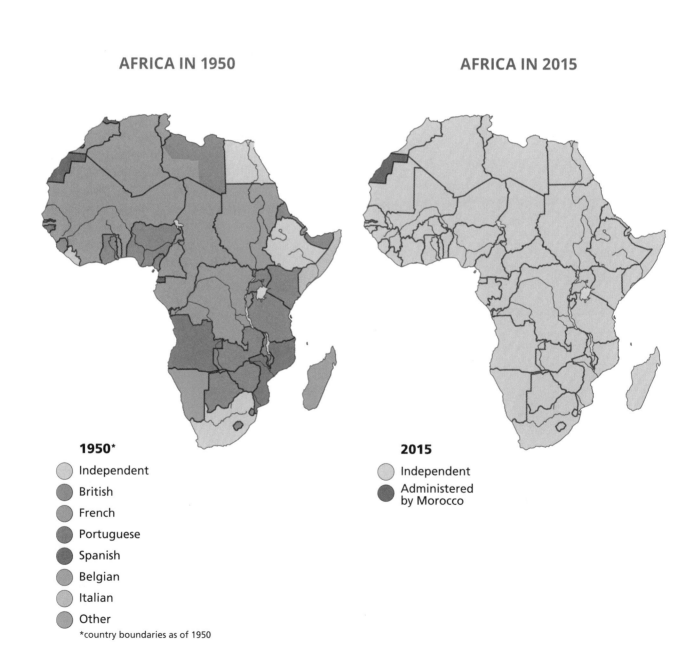

AFRICA IN 1950

AFRICA IN 2015

1950*
- Independent
- British
- French
- Portuguese
- Spanish
- Belgian
- Italian
- Other

*country boundaries as of 1950

2015
- Independent
- Administered by Morocco

Crack the code to write the Swahili name of each African animal.

1	2	3	4	5	6	7	8	9	10	11	12	13	14
F	M	A	C	S	U	T	G	H	I	B	W	D	L

F I S I
1 10 5 10

D U M A
13 6 2 3

T W I G A
7 12 10 8 3

S W A L A
5 12 3 14 3

S I M B A
5 10 2 11 3

C H A T U
4 9 3 7 6

The **Sahara** is the world's largest desert. It stretches from the Atlantic Ocean to the Red Sea in northern Africa. The Sahara, like other deserts, gets little rainfall, and it can get very hot during the day—sometimes as high as 130 degrees Fahrenheit (55 degrees Celsius). That's almost as hot as a sauna!

In the center of Africa near the equator are tropical **rain forest** areas. The rain forests are hot and humid and have dense, tangled trees and plants.

AFRICA: ENVIRONMENT

Legend

- Forest
- Swamp
- Cropland and woodland
- Cropland
- Crop and grazing land
- Grassland
- Desert
- Urban

You already know about deserts and rain forests. Here are some terms for other African environments, which don't appear on the map on the opposite page.

Oasis—An area in the desert that has water and plants.

Sahel—The semiarid, or partly dry, area just south of the Sahara.

Savanna—Grassy plains with a few trees; in North America, this same environment is called a prairie.

Write each of the words below in the correct spot on the puzzle. One letter has already been filled in to get you started.

sahel

oasis

jungle

desert

savanna

equator

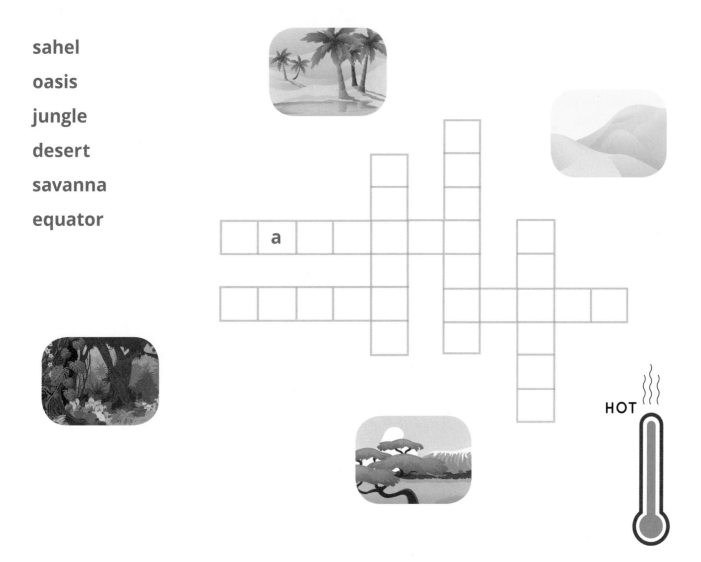

Nearly half of the world's diamonds can be found in Africa. Diamonds are mined from the ground, then cut, polished, and shipped around the world. Diamonds are one of the hardest materials on Earth. They are so hard that they can cut through glass and steel.

Africa began mining diamonds in the late 1800s. At that time, slaves did the work. Today, there is still controversy about the way the laborers in diamond mines are treated. Many countries in Africa also mine gold, and some mine copper and iron too.

AFRICA: DIAMONDS

Legend

Diamond mines

Unscramble the letters below to form the names of five African countries. Then unscramble the circled letters to complete the sentence.

1. R E A R I S N E(E)L O _____

2. L A(N)G O A _____

3. H O U T(S) F R A C I A _____

4. U A N G E(I) _____

5. W A B E(M)B I Z _____

_____

These countries all have diamond ___ ___ ___ ___ ___ .

Who Knew?

A Diamond Fit for a King
The world's largest cut diamond is called the Golden Jubilee Diamond. It was given to the king of Thailand in 1996 to celebrate his 50-year reign as king.

Imagine traveling in a hot air balloon across southern Africa, starting in Zambia. As you cross the border to Zimbabwe, you see a huge waterfall–**Victoria Falls**, one of the seven natural wonders of the world!

In Zimbabwe you also see **Mutarazi Falls**, the second-highest falls in Africa. To get to the highest falls on the continent, you guide your balloon to **Tugela Falls** in South Africa. These waterfalls are the world's second-tallest. In South Africa you also see **Mpumalanga Falls**.

You continue to Lesotho, a small country surrounded by South Africa. Here you spot **Maletsungame Falls**, which is three times higher than Niagara Falls. As you head north again, the balloon floats over the Tanzania-Zambia border, where you take in **Kalambo Falls**.

SOUTHERN AFRICA: WATERFALLS

Take another balloon ride, this time starting in Lesotho and traveling south to north. Write the order of the countries you will pass over as you travel from south to north. Use the text and the map on the opposite page to help you.

5. _____

4. _____

3. _____

2. _____

1. _____

The **Middle East** is not a continent, but an area where three continents meet—Africa, Asia, and Europe. In ancient times, there was a land called Mesopotamia where the Middle Eastern countries of Iraq, Turkey, and part of Syria now lie. Mesopotamia is sometimes called the "cradle of civilization" because some of the world's earliest settlements were there. "Mesopotamia" means "land between the rivers." Can you find the two rivers on the map?

MIDDLE EAST

Find the names of Middle Eastern countries using only the letters in the cube. You don't need all of the letters for each name, but you can't use any letters that aren't in the cube. Each letter can be used only once in each name. Use the map on the opposite page to help you, and look at the example before you start.

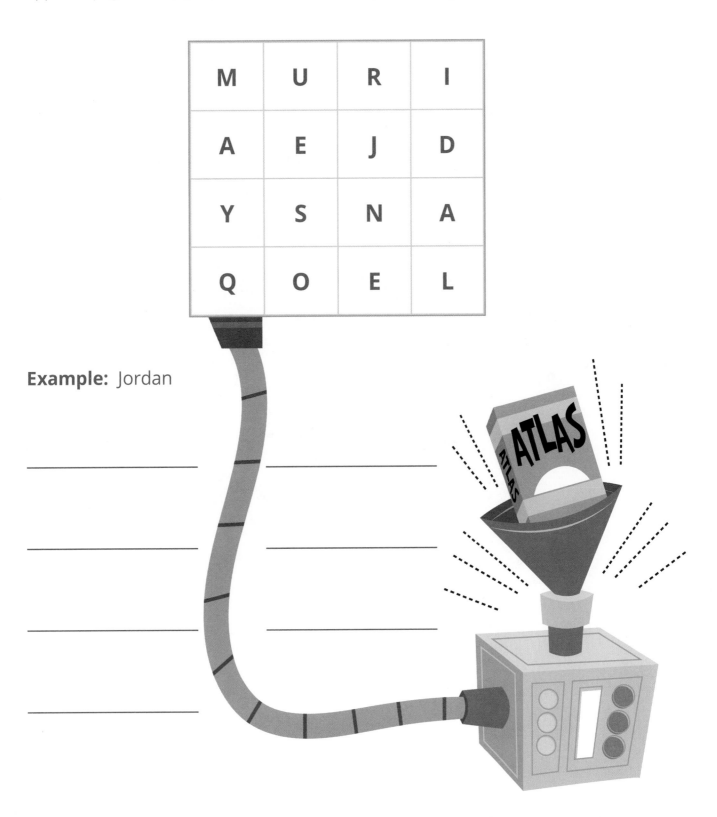

M	U	R	I
A	E	J	D
Y	S	N	A
Q	O	E	L

Example: Jordan

_____ _____

_____ _____

_____ _____

_____

The land of the **Middle East** is rich in oil, but it's not rich in another liquid: water. Much of the land here is dry and desert-like. Three rivers help people live in this hot climate—the **Tigris**, the **Euphrates**, and the **Nile**.

The Nile is the longest river in the world. It stretches for more than 4,000 miles. Until 2004, no one had ever navigated its entire length!

The Tigris and the Euphrates rivers flow north to south into the Persian Gulf, passing through Syria and Iraq. Like the Nile, these rivers help make the land around them fertile and good for farming.

MIDDLE EAST

Who Knew?

Roadblock at Sea
The Suez Canal allows ships to travel from the Mediterranean Sea to the Red Sea. During the 1967 war between Egypt and Israel, Egypt sunk ships in the Suez Canal to block traffic.

Fill in the middle row of river pebbles with the names of the Middle Eastern countries each river flows through. Then fill in the bottom pebble with the name of the body of water each river flows into.

Euphrates

Tigris

Nile

Asia is the largest continent. It reaches all the way from the Arctic Circle to the country of Indonesia on the equator, and more than half of the world's people live there.

Besides having a lot of people, Asia also has a lot of variations in climate. In Siberia, a region of Russia, winter lasts seven to eight months! But Indonesia is steamy and tropical.

Asia is the home of the world's highest mountain, Mt. Everest. In the language of Nepal, it's called the "Forehead in the Sky."

Fill in the puzzle using the clues below.

Across

3. If you forgot the name of this southernmost Asian country, you'd have amnesia about _____ .

4. This is a large country in Asia, not to mention the plate you eat your dinner from.

5. Considering how long it takes to reach the top, maybe this mountain should be called "Ever-climb."

6. It's not the Arctic Square; it's the _____ Circle.

Down

1. Asia is the largest of all of these.

2. Even though this place is really cold, it's not spelled "Sibrrria."

Who Knew?

A Heck of a Hike
The oldest person to climb Mt. Everest was 80 years old. The youngest boy, 13 years old, reached the summit in 2010. In 2013, the youngest girl, also 13 years old, reached the summit.

Strong-smelling spices, street vendors selling fruits and vegetables, brightly colored fabrics, and people shouting are some of the things you might smell, see, and hear in a busy village market in India, the largest country in southern Asia. One of the most populated cities in the world is in **India**—Mumbai.

The Arabian Sea borders India on the west, and the Bay of Bengal borders India on the east. The Ganges River runs through northern India. The Himalayas border India to the north. Can you find these water and land features on the map below?

INDIA

Legend
⊛ Capital
● City
— Country boundary

Who am I? Read each clue and write down the answer.

1. I am one of the world's most crowded cities. _____

2. I am a country that borders India to the west. _____

3. The Ganges River flows into me. _____

4. I am a small country located between two parts of India in the northeast corner and I border the Bay of Bengal.

   _____

5. I am India's capital city. _____

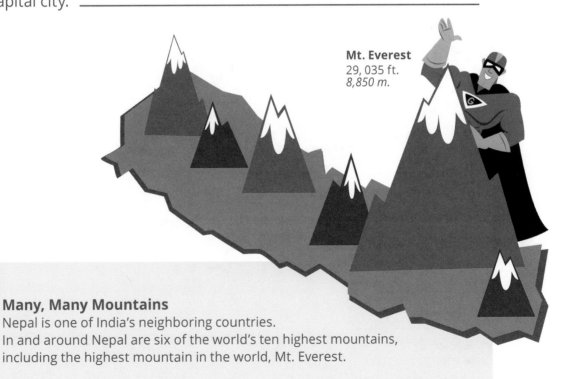

Mt. Everest
29, 035 ft.
8,850 m.

Who Knew?

Many, Many Mountains
Nepal is one of India's neighboring countries.
In and around Nepal are six of the world's ten highest mountains,
including the highest mountain in the world, Mt. Everest.

China is the third-largest country in the world, after Russia and Canada, but it has the largest number of people. Its population is so large that cities are very crowded. Since the cities are so crowded, most people travel by foot or bicycle rather than by car.

Most of China's people live in the eastern part of the country, which has rich farmland for growing crops such as rice and tea. The Yangtze River, one of the longest rivers in the world, flows west to east through the country.

CHINA

Legend

⊛ Capital
● City
— Country boundary

China has many countries that border it on all sides. First study the map on the opposite page. Then try to name all of China's neighbors on the lines below.

_____

_____

N

_____

_____

W   E   _____

_____

S

_____

_____

_____

_____

_____

80 POUNDS

Who Knew?

Pass the Bamboo
Giant pandas live in China. Pandas eat bamboo—lots of it. A panda eats about 80 pounds (36 kilograms) of bamboo stems, shoots, and leaves each day. Because so much bamboo has been cut down to make way for human settlement, the giant pandas are in danger of disappearing.

Lying off the coast of mainland Asia, **Japan** is made up of thousands of islands, most of which are too small to see on the map below. The four main islands are Hokkaido, Honshu, Shikoku, and Kyushu.

Much of Japan is mountainous, so most of its people live in busy cities along the coast. Most of the major cities are located on the island of Honshu.

The city of Kobe is famous for its expensive, high-quality beef. Tokyo, Japan's capital, is very crowded and has one of the best public transportation systems in the world. Japan is known throughout the world for making cars, many of which are manufactured in the city of Nagoya.

JAPAN

China

Russia

Sapporo

Hokkaido

North Korea

Sea of Japan (East Sea)

South Korea

Honshu

Japan

Mount Fuji

Tokyo

Kyoto

Yokohama

Kobe

Nagoya

Osaka

Shikoku

Kyushu

PACIFIC OCEAN

N NE NW E W SW SE S

Legend

⊛ Capital
● City
— Country boundary

Circle these Japanese cities on the map, and then circle their names in the word search puzzle below.

Kobe

Tokyo

Kyoto

Yokohama

Nagoya

Sapporo

P	S	K	U	T	V	M	L
N	Q	R	Y	W	O	N	A
A	M	A	H	O	K	O	Y
G	O	C	H	Y	T	E	Z
O	K	X	J	K	I	O	M
Y	E	Y	K	O	B	E	A
A	R	E	I	T	U	Y	I
S	A	P	P	O	R	O	S

Time Yourself!

BEST TIME: _____min. _____sec.

Who Knew?

Different City, Same Letters
You can rearrange the letters of the current capital city of Japan—Tokyo—to get the name of the former capital city—Kyoto.

Many people in Southeast Asia live in villages, where they farm rice and other crops with the help of the water buffalo, a large, strong animal that can plow fields. Other southeast Asian animals include the Asian elephant and the mouse deer, a kind of deer that is only about as big as a dog or cat! This region has important urban centers, too, such as the city of Manila in the Philippines.

Southeast Asia has a hot climate, green forests, and sandy beaches, which makes it attractive to tourists. However, this region also has a rainy monsoon season from June to October and some of the world's most active volcanoes.

SOUTHEAST ASIA

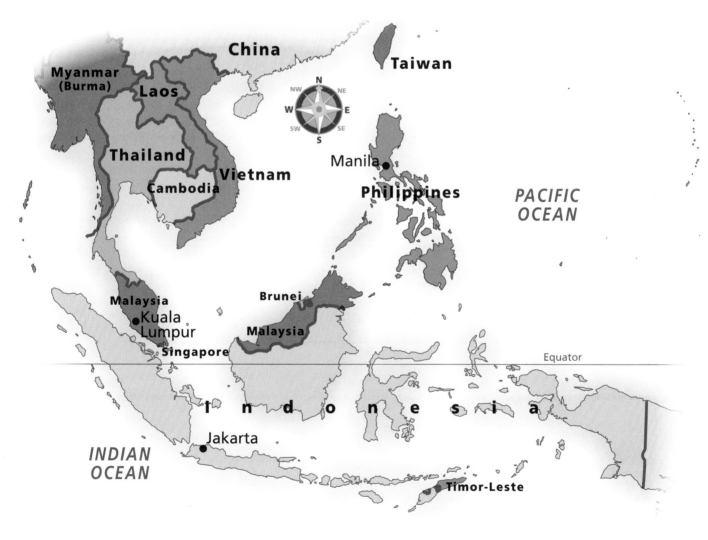

Legend

● City
— Country boundary

Fill in the blanks to complete this tourism poster advertising the countries of southeast Asia. Use the information on the opposite page to help you.

VISIT BEAUTIFUL SOUTHEAST ASIA!

Enjoy our sandy _____ and our

_____ climate.

If you're lucky, you'll see interesting animals such as the

_____ and the _____ .

Just be sure to visit during the months of

_____ to _____

and not during our rainy season, which is called the

_____ season.

Australia is the only continent, except for Antarctica, that is located completely in the southern hemisphere. Because it lies "under" the equator, people often call it the land "down under."

Australia is about the size of the 48 contiguous, or joined, states of the United States. It is divided into six states and two territories. It is the smallest continent, and it is also a country. The native people of Australia are called **Aborigines**.

Most people live in the southeastern part of Australia, especially near the big cities Sydney, Melbourne, Adelaide, and Canberra, the nation's capital.

AUSTRALIA

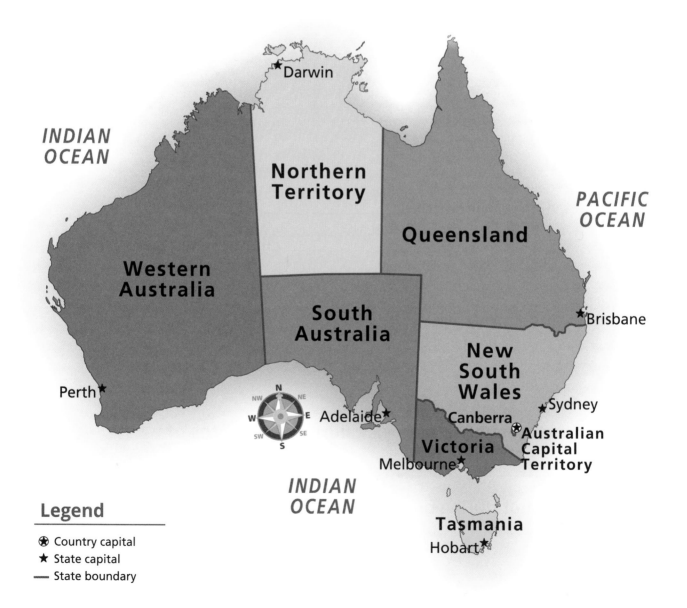

Legend

- ⊛ Country capital
- ★ State capital
- — State boundary

How well do you know Australia? Write the names of each of the states and territories on the lines below, and then match each one with its capital city.

_____

_____

_____

_____

_____

_____

_____

_____

- **Canberra**

- **Perth**

- **Brisbane**

- **Darwin**

- **Melbourne**

- **Sydney**

- **Adelaide**

- **Hobart**

Who Knew?

Let's Celebrate!
Every year in April, Australians celebrate National Youth Week. It's a week of sports, concerts, festivals, and talent competitions for young people ages 12 to 25.

What do koalas and kangaroos have in common? For one thing, you won't find them anywhere outside Australia (except, of course, for zoos). Also, kangaroos and koalas both carry their babies in a pouch, and both kangaroo babies and koala babies are called joeys. And they both belong to the group of animals called marsupials.

Koalas may look cuddly, but they have strong jaws and sharp claws. Some people call them "koala bears," but they're really not bears at all. They sleep about 20 hours a day.

Australia has more than 60 different types of kangaroos, but the most common is the red kangaroo. They can hop more than 40 miles (70 kilometers) an hour. By comparison, a very, very fast human can run about 13 miles (about 21 kilometers) an hour.

AUSTRALIA

With the exception of the Australian Capital Territory, there is an official (or unofficial) animal for each state or territory. Use the clues to discover which animal belongs where. Write the letter of each animal on the line beside its description.

A — **Platypus** B — **Red Kangaroo** C — **Koala** D — **Hairy-nosed Wombat** E — **Tasmanian Devil** F — **Leadbeater's Possum** G — **Numbat**

‑ ‑ ‑ ‑ ‑ ‑ ‑   ‑ ‑ ‑ ‑ ‑ ‑ ‑   ‑ ‑ ‑ ‑ ‑ ‑ ‑

1. **Tasmania**—Our animal can cause trouble, but we gave it our name anyway. _____

2. **Queensland**—We know our animal is not a bear, but we can "bear-ly" live without it. _____

3. **New South Wales**—Our animal has a duck-like face and webbed feet. _____

4. **Western Australia**—Our animal looks like an anteater. _____

5. **South Australia**—This animal is named for its furry snout. _____

6. **Northern Territory**—Ours is the best-known 'roo in Australia. (From her name, you might think that she's blushing all over!) _____

7. **Victoria**—Our creature is wee and lives in a tree. _____

Who Knew?

Thirsty?
The name koala comes from an Aboriginal word that means "no drink." Koalas get most of the liquid that they need from eucalyptus leaves, which is the only thing they eat.

Dry and dusty—these are two words that describe much of Australia's landscape. Although the country is a large island, most of the land is desert-like. Australians call this dry land the Outback.

Crops, people, and animals find it difficult to live in the Outback, yet some do. Many of Australia's sheep and cattle farms, or stations, can be found in the outback. **Uluru** (also known as Ayers Rock), one of Australia's famous natural landmarks, is located in the dry lands of central Australia. It is considered the world's largest single stone. From a distance, it appears to glow bright red!

AUSTRALIA: ENVIRONMENTS

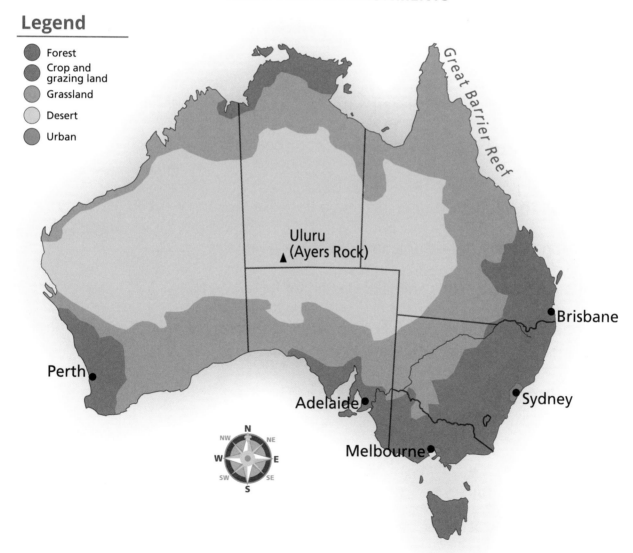

Legend
- Forest
- Crop and grazing land
- Grassland
- Desert
- Urban

This or that? Circle the underlined words that are the best answers for each question. Use the map and the information on the opposite page to help you.

1. Is more of Australia's desert located in the continent's <u>northwest</u> or <u>southeast</u> region?

2. If you owned a sheep station in the Outback, would your station most likely be found near <u>Melbourne</u> or <u>Uluru</u> (Ayers Rock)?

3. Much of Australia is desert-like land. Would you say $\frac{1}{10}$ or $\frac{1}{2}$ of Australia is desert-like land?

4. Which city is closer to the Australian desert, <u>Perth</u> or <u>Melbourne</u>?

5. Are Australia's busy urban, or city, areas in Australia's <u>northeast</u> or <u>southeast</u> region?

Who Knew?

Little but large
The biggest living thing on earth isn't an elephant or a whale. It's the Great Barrier Reef, which runs for about 1,250 miles (2,000 kilometers) off the eastern coast of Australia. The reef is made of countless tiny animals called coral polyps, which produce limestone to form an external skeleton for themselves.

English is the official language of Australia, but there are also many languages spoken by Australia's native people, known as Aborigines. At one time there were more than 100 Aboriginal languages, but many have now died out. However, many familiar Australian words, such as kangaroo, come from Aboriginal words. Others are just slang words that the Australians have invented.

A friend is a mate or a cobber, and if you want to greet someone, you say, "G'day, mate!" In the bubbles below, you can learn some Australian words. Try them out on your friends!

Can you speak Australian? Draw lines to match the word on the right with the definition on the left. Look at the map on the opposite page if you need help.

strides

chewie

sanger (cut lunch)

sunnies

alligator pear

bathers

chokkie

- chocolate
- sandwich
- trousers
- avocado
- swimsuit
- sunglasses
- gum

When is a kiwi not a bird or a fruit? When it's a New Zealander instead! The residents of this island country, which lies about 1,000 miles (1,600 kilometers) southeast of Australia, refer to themselves as Kiwis after the flightless kiwi bird that lives there. Most New Zealanders live on North Island, many of them in the capital, Wellington, or in the largest city, Auckland. Native New Zealanders are known as Maoris.

Oceania is the name of a group of islands in the south Pacific Ocean. The three main groups of islands in Oceania are Melanesia, Micronesia, and Polynesia. The weather here is warm year-round. Sometimes Australia and New Zealand are considered part of Oceania, too.

NEW ZEALAND AND OCEANIA

Micronesia

Hawaiian Islands

Melanesia

Polynesia

Australia

PACIFIC OCEAN

Tasman Sea

Auckland · North Island

South Island · Wellington

New Zealand

Legend

⊛ Country capital
● City
— Country boundary

Find the two major islands of New Zealand on the map on the opposite page, and write their names on the lines below.

_____

_____

What are Oceania's three main groups of islands?

_____

_____

_____

Some of the words on the opposite page are hidden in the puzzle below. Circle them.

Auckland   **New Zealand**   **Oceania**   **Wellington**   **Pacific**   **Maori**

D	N	A	L	K	C	U	A	N	H
N	W	L	C	N	O	W	V	E	I
A	E	P	V	A	N	O	X	W	K
L	L	M	A	O	R	I	L	U	J
A	L	R	O	C	S	K	L	E	P
E	I	F	P	A	I	T	D	R	T
Z	N	P	I	U	V	F	E	P	C
W	G	O	C	E	A	N	I	A	D
E	T	L	F	I	C	T	D	C	A
N	O	S	T	A	Z	C	F	O	O
B	N	A	O	P	X	W	E	T	E

"The Ice" is a common nickname for **Antarctica**. That's because it is almost completely covered in it. Antarctica is the coldest, windiest place on Earth. It is also the driest and the most uninhabitable. No one lives on Antarctica permanently. Antarctica is the home of the southernmost spot on Earth—the South Pole.

In the summer, which lasts only from November to January, some of the Antarctic ice melts, but it's still very cold. In Eastern Antarctica, where it's coldest, the average temperature is –27 degrees Fahrenheit (–33 degrees Celsius) even in the warmest months. In the winter, Antarctica doubles in size because of the ice that forms around its coasts.

ANTARCTICA

Who am I? Read each clue and write the answer.

1. I am a stretch of land that juts out into the ocean toward South America.

_____

2. I am the southernmost spot on Earth. _____

3. I am a mountain range that spans the continent. _____

4. I am a large body of water that surrounds Antarctica. _____

5. I am a land that lies between Victoria Land and Enderby Land.

_____

Who Knew?

Not a Drop to Drink
The ice sheet that covers nearly all of Antarctica holds 90 percent of all the ice on earth. But the entire continent gets only about two inches (50 millimeters) of rain and snow a year, making it one of the biggest deserts in the world!

At Home in Antarctica

Antarctica's cold, harsh weather means that the continent has no towns, roads, schools, hospitals, or stores! But it has one thing: scientists. Many countries from around the world have scientific research stations in Antarctica.

At research stations, scientists study the sea, ice, and Antarctic environment. Transportation to and from Antarctica—usually by air—can happen only from November through January. That's the only time that supplies can arrive, too. In other months, blizzards, wind, and ice make it impossible.

ANTARCTICA: SCIENTIFIC STATIONS

Legend

● Scientific station

In the blanks below, write the letter of the station that matches the location.

A. Amundsen-Scott Station   **C. Neumayer Station**   **E. Casey Base**

B. Vostok Station   **D. Esperanza Station**

1. Located on Antarctic Peninsula   _____

2. Located nearest the South Pole   _____

3. Australian station on the coast   _____

4. Russian station located inland   _____

5. Located closest to Halley Station   _____

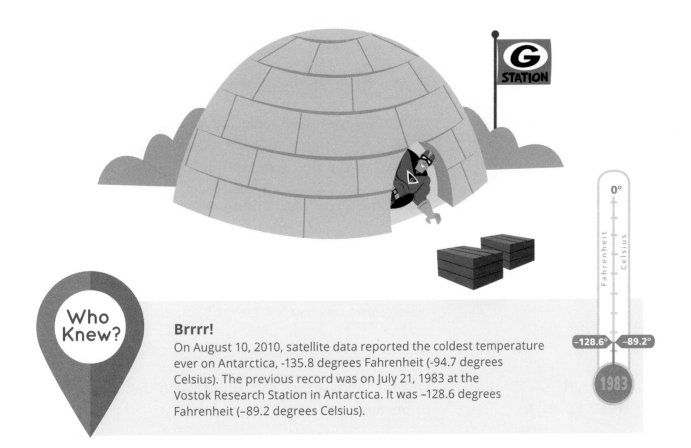

Who Knew?

Brrrr!
On August 10, 2010, satellite data reported the coldest temperature ever on Antarctica, -135.8 degrees Fahrenheit (-94.7 degrees Celsius). The previous record was on July 21, 1983 at the Vostok Research Station in Antarctica. It was –128.6 degrees Fahrenheit (–89.2 degrees Celsius).

altitude	height above sea level
bar scale	the part of a map that tells how much distance on Earth is shown by each inch or centimeter on a map
bingo key	a letter and number combination, such as A-4, that is assigned to a particular section on a map
boundary	an imaginary line that divides one area of land from another; also called a border
capital	the city where state, province, or national government leaders work
cardinal directions	North, East, South, West
Celsius	one type of scale used to measure temperature; named after the Swedish astronomer who created it
climate	an area's average daily weather conditions; temperature, precipitation, distance from the equator, and distance from the sea help form an area's climate
climate map	a map that shows the kind of weather a place has
compass rose	symbol on a map that shows directions
contiguous states	name given to the 48 joined states of the United States that are part of one landmass; Alaska and Hawaii are not part of the contiguous 48 states.
continent	one of the seven large landmasses on Earth: North America, South America, Europe, Africa, Asia, Australia, and Antarctica
country	an area of land that is separated from others by political borders and has its own government and citizens
desert	a large, dry area of land
Eastern Hemisphere	all land and water on the half of Earth that is east of the prime meridian

elevation	the height above the ground or above sea level
environment	an area's surroundings
environment map	a type of thematic map that shows different environments of a particular area
equator	a line on a map that divides the Northern Hemisphere from the Southern Hemisphere
Eurasia	name given to the shared landmass of Europe and Asia
Fahrenheit	one type of scale used to measure temperature; named after the German physicist who created it
glacier	a large, slow-moving body of ice
globe	a model of Earth shaped like a sphere, or ball, just like Earth
Greenwich	the time at the prime meridian at 0 degrees longitude, located in Greenwich, England
hemisphere	half the earth
intermediate directions	Northeast, Southeast, Northwest, Southwest
International Date Line	an imaginary line at 180 degrees longitude in the Pacific Ocean marking the boundary between one day and the next
island	land that is surrounded by water
land use map	a type of thematic map that shows how an area of land is being used
landform	a physical feature on the earth's surface with a recognizable shape, such as a mountain or valley
landmass	a large body of land

latitude	lines that run east and west on a map or globe that measure the distance from the Equator in degrees
legend	the part of a map that tells what the symbols, lines, and other pictures on a map mean
longitude	lines that run north and south on a map or globe that measure the distance from the prime meridian in degrees
map	a flat drawing of Earth's surface
map grid	a system of letters and numbers on a map that can be used to locate places
map scale	the way distances on a map compare to real distances on Earth
Northern Hemisphere	All land and water on the half of Earth that is north of the equator
ocean	one of the five main bodies of water on Earth
peninsula	land that is almost surrounded by water
physical features	features on Earth made by nature
physical map	a map that shows physical features and often shows the height of land and the depth of oceans
political map	a map that shows how people have divided the land
population map	a map that shows the number of people who live in an area
precipitation	rain, snow, sleet, hail
prime meridian	the line that, along with the 180 degree line of longitude, divides the Eastern Hemisphere from the Western Hemisphere
projection	a way of showing, or projecting, Earth's surface, which is round, as a flat drawing

province	an area of a country that is separated by boundaries and shares a national government with the other provinces or territories of the country
rain forest	one of the wettest places on Earth; a rain forest receives at least 100 inches (254 centimeters) of rain a year
regions	places that have something in common, such as climate, culture, or traditions
road map	a map that shows highways and streets
sea	a large body of salt water that is smaller than an ocean
source	the place where a river starts
Southern Hemisphere	All land and water on the half of Earth that is south of the equator
state	an area of a country that is separated by boundaries and shares a national government with the other states or territories of the country
state boundary	the line on a map that shows where a state begins or ends
symbol	a line, color, or shape on a map that stands for something else
territory	an area of land that belongs to or is controlled by someone or something, such as a country's government
thematic map	a type of map that shows special kinds of information about a place, such as climate or population
time zone	one of the parts of Earth that have the same time in common; most time zones have a time that is one hour different from the zones next to it
Western Hemisphere	All land and water on the half of Earth that is west of the prime meridian

STATE ABBREVIATIONS

AK	Alaska	MT	Montana
AL	Alabama	NC	North Carolina
AR	Arkansas	ND	North Dakota
AZ	Arizona	NE	Nebraska
CA	California	NH	New Hampshire
CO	Colorado	NJ	New Jersey
CT	Connecticut	NM	New Mexico
DE	Delaware	NV	Nevada
DC	District of Columbia	NY	New York
FL	Florida	OH	Ohio
GA	Georgia	OK	Oklahoma
HI	Hawaii	OR	Oregon
IA	Iowa	PA	Pennsylvania
ID	Idaho	RI	Rhode Island
IL	Illinois	SC	South Carolina
IN	Indiana	SD	South Dakota
KS	Kansas	TN	Tennessee
KY	Kentucky	TX	Texas
LA	Louisiana	UT	Utah
MA	Massachusetts	VT	Vermont
MD	Maryland	VA	Virginia
ME	Maine	WA	Washington
MI	Michigan	WI	Wisconsin
MN	Minnesota	WV	West Virginia
MO	Missouri	WY	Wyoming
MS	Mississippi		

Answers

Page 5
1. Hiking area
2. Playground
3. Bridge

Page 7
1. South
2. Northwest
3. Southeast
4. West

Page 9
1. Denver
2. Vail
3. A-1
4. Black Canyon of the Gunnison National Park

Page 11
1. About 10 miles or about 20 kilometers
2. About 50 miles or about 80 kilometers
3. False
4. Springville
5. West Ridge
6. About 20 miles or about 35 kilometers

Page 13
One map is oval, and one is rectangular.

The vertical lines in the map grid on the Robinson projection are curved, and on the Miller projection they're straight.

In the Miller projection, Antarctica looks much bigger that it does on the Robinson projection.

The continents in the Miller projection look wider than in the Robinson projection.

Page 15
1. 1,000
2. 2,000 bushels = 2 apple symbols
3. 10,000
4. 23,000
5. Half an apple

Page 17
1. desert
2. landforms
3. elevation
4. plains
5. boundary
6. height
7. ocean
8. natural

Page 21
1. East
2. Texas
3. Nevada
4. Hawaii

Page 23
1. desert
2. precipitation
3. equator
4. climate map
5. climate

Page 25
Statements 2, 5, and 6 are false.

Page 27

Across	Down
2. urban	1. tundra
4. desert	3. grassland
6. swamp	5. thematic
7. cropland	

Page 29
1. North America and Europe
2. Australia and Antarctica
3. North America and South America
4. Australia
5. Europe, Africa, Asia

Page 31
1. hot
4. dry
5. yes

Page 33
Arctic Ocean: The northernmost ocean
Antarctica: The southernmost continent (Penguins love it!)
South America: The continent south of North America
Indian Ocean: One of the oceans that surrounds Africa
Asia: The largest continent
Australia: The smallest continent (It's also a country!)

Page 35
1. Madagascar
2. Sudan
3. Libya
4. Algeria
5. Congo

Page 37
- London, 8 a.m. Thursday: New York, 3 a.m. Thursday; Paris, 9 a.m. Thursday; Sydney, 6 p.m. Thursday
- Mexico City, 5 p.m. Thursday: New York, 6 p.m. Thursday; Paris, 12 a.m. Friday; Sydney, 9 a.m. Friday
- Tokyo, midnight Thursday: New York, 10 a.m. Wednesday; Paris, 4 p.m. Wednesday; Sydney, 1 a.m. Thursday

Page 39
1. T
2. F
3. F
4. F
5. F
6. T

Page 41
Yukon, bordered by British Columbia and Northwest Territories
Manitoba, bordered by Ontario, Nunavut, and Saskatchewan
Québec, bordered by Newfoundland and Labrador, New Brunswick, and Ontario

Page 43
1. Québec
2. Iqaluit
3. Hudson Bay
4. Northwest Territories, Manitoba
5. English and French

Page 45

Down	Across
1. Montana	3. Virginia
2. Georgia	4. Ohio
3. Vermont	5. Utah
6. Arizona	

Page 47
Regions named for physical features: Rocky Mountains, Great Plains
Regions named for oceans: Pacific, Mid-Atlantic
Regions named for directions: Southwest, South, Midwest, Northeast

Page 49
1. Connecticut
2. Delaware
3. Maryland
4. Massachusetts
5. New Jersey
6. New Hampshire
7. New York
8. Rhode Island
9. Pennsylvania
GA = Georgia; NC = North Carolina;
SC = South Carolina; VA = Virginia

Page 51
1. Michigan
2. Superior
3. Erie
Minnesota, Wisconsin, Michigan, Illinois, Indiana, Ohio

Page 53
South: humid, beaches, some states border ocean
Southwest: dry, canyons, desert
Both: hot, popular with tourists

Page 57
1. The United Mexican States
2. Spanish
3. Mexico City
4. The United States, Belize, Guatemala
5. 31
6. The Pacific Ocean

Page 59

Across	Down
1. Acapulco	2. factories
3. grapes	4. silver
5. Ixtapa	6. north
	7. Cancun

Page 61
1. Belize, Guatemala
2. Panama
3. Honduras, Costa Rica
4. El Salvador
5. Bahamas
6. An island

Page 63
1. Havana
2. San Juan
3. Santo Domingo
4. Port-au-Prince
5. Kingston
6. Nassau

Page 67
Mountain
1. False
2. Andes Mountains
3. They have thick woolly coats.
River basin
1. False
2. Shallow
3. The Amazon River Basin

Page 69
1. 25 pounds of bananas
2. 40 pounds of oranges and 5 pounds of bananas
3. 50 pounds of coffee beans and 20 pounds of oranges
4. 1,000 pounds of sugarcane

Page 73
Ecuador: Sangay, Cotopaxi, Sumaco
Chile: Cerro Azul, Copahue, Villarrica
Colombia: Tolima, Huila, Galeras

Page 75
1. Spain
2. Turkey
3. Ukraine
4. Iceland
5. Sweden

Page 77
From London to Paris: English Channel
From Rome to Madrid: Mediterranean Sea
From Venice to Athens: Adriatic Sea
From Dublin to London: Irish Sea

Page 79
1. Alps
2. Cantabrian
3. Pyrenees
4. Apennines
5. Caucasus
6. Carpathian
7. Ural

Page 81

Across	Down
1. Colosseum	1. castles
2. Stonehenge	3. Eiffel Tower
4. Acropolis	5. landmark
6. windmills	
7. Rhine	

Page 83
United Kingdom: Cheddar
Netherlands: Gouda
Germany: Limburger
Switzerland: Swiss
France: Brie
Spain: Cabrales
Italy: Mozzarella
Hungary: Trappista
Greece: Feta

Page 85

Algeria or Angola
SOUTH AFRICA
Rwanda
ZAIRE
Chad
Angola or Algeria
NIGER

Congo
MOROCCO
Namibia or Nigeria
Togo
LIBERIA
Nigeria or Namibia
Egypt
SENEGAL
Tunisia

Page 87
hyena: fisi; cheetah: duma; giraffe: twiga; impala: swala;
python: chatu; lion: simba

Page 91
1. Sierra Leone
2. Angola
3. South Africa
4. Guinea
5. Zimbabwe
These countries all have diamond mines.

Page 93
1. Lesotho
2. South Africa
3. Zimbabwe
4. Zambia
5. Tanzania

Page 95
Syria, Israel, Sudan, Yemen, Oman, Iran, Iraq

Page 97
The Euphrates flows through Turkey, Syria, and Iraq and into
the Persian Gulf.
The Tigris flows through Turkey, Syria, and Iraq and into the
Persian Gulf.
The Nile flows through Sudan and Egypt and into the
Mediterranean Sea.

Page 99

Across	Down
3. Indonesia	1. continents
4. China	2. Siberia
5. Everest	
6. Arctic	

Page 101
1. Mumbai
2. Pakistan
3. Bay of Bengal

4. Bangladesh
5. New Delhi

Page 103
North: Mongolia, Russia
East: North Korea
South: Vietnam, Laos, Myanmar, Bhutan, Nepal, India
West: Kazakhstan, Pakistan, Afghanistan, Tajikistan,
Kyrgyzstan

Page 107
Enjoy our sandy beaches and our hot climate.
If you're lucky, you'll see interesting animals such as the
Asian elephant and the mouse deer.
Just be sure to visit during the months of November to
May and not during our rainy season, which is called the
monsoon season.

Page 109
Western Australia: Perth
Northern Territory: Darwin
South Australia: Adelaide
Queensland: Brisbane
New South Wales: Sydney
Victoria: Melbourne
Australian Capital Territory: Canberra
Tasmania: Hobart

Page 111
1. E
2. C
3. A
4. G
5. D
6. B
7. F

Page 113
1. northwest
2. Uluru
3. 12
4. Perth
5. southeast

Page 115
Strides = trousers
Chewie = gum
Sanger (cut lunch) = sandwich
Sunnies = sunglasses
Alligator pear = avocado
Bathers = swimsuit
Chokkie = chocolate

Page 117
North Island
South Island
Melanesia
Micronesia
Polynesia

Page 119
1. Antarctic Peninsula
2. South Pole
3. Transantarctic Mountains
4. Southern Ocean
5. Wilkes Land

Page 121
1. D
2. A
3. E
4. B
5. C